Leaders Recommend *Connect the Dots... To Become an Impact Player:*

Connect the Dots *is a reminder to all of us to reach for the sky until you get burnt. Then, instead of turning back, it urges us to keep reaching with a better understanding of how to avoid that same heat. Dick Lynch has skillfully combined education with inspiration.*

—Chris Berman, sportscaster, ESPN

Connect the Dots *provides the reader with a roadmap to effective leadership. By demonstrating principles and theories that work, I believe Lynch has captured what it takes to be a leader. His key principles are universally applicable—whether it's in public service, business, or in our daily lives.*

—Rob Portman, United States Representative

Connect the Dots, *written by Dick Lynch, is an excellent book on leadership. Everyone wants to excel in leadership and Dick has some exceptional ideas that I have not read before. I learned a lot from this fine book.*

—Bobby Bowden, head football coach, Florida State University

This book should be a must-read from the classroom to the boardroom. Dick Lynch has captured those very important messages we all want to pass along to our children about life, commitment, leadership, and citizenship. It's about how to live a life worth living.

—Larry D. Savage, president & CEO, Humana of Ohio

If you want to maximize your proficiency in change leadership, then read Connect the Dots—*today!*

—Dick Lyles, author, *Winning Ways*

In this book, Mr. Lynch has captured the essence of leadership, i.e., the realization of vision through discipline dedicated to making a positive difference in the lives of others. Vision is the catalyst...discipline is the determining factor in the equation of successful leadership.

—Wm. T. (Bill) Robinson III, Esq., Greenebaum Doll McDonald, chair of the finance committee and member of executive committee, American Bar Association Board of Governors

Connect the Dots *is a worthwhile fast read, in the best sense of fast read—clear and engrossing. The core of the book is the interviews—an uncommon opportunity to learn important and useful ideas from high achievement leaders.*

—Barrett Hazeltine, professor emeritus of engineering, Brown University

My definition of success is learning to turn the fear of failure into an effective exercise of positive completion. Obviously, the leaders interviewed in Connect the Dots *are successful people that everyone in society can learn from.*

—Clark Gaines, senior regional director, NFL Players Association

As investors in entrepreneurial companies, we look for impact players. This readable little treasure reminds us all of what a difference they can make—in a business, and in their community and, in some cases, their country. Would-be entrepreneurs should sit down and read this—but so should anyone who strives to make a difference in other peoples' lives.

—Hap Ellis, partner, Rockport Capital Partners

Dick has brought an impressive group of successful business leaders together and provided truly wonderful advice and commentary from worldwide leaders to produce a great motivational treatise on leadership and success. I recommend it highly.

—Jay Kern, managing director, Reynolds, DeWitt & Co

Dick Lynch has ushered in a new generation of thought on leadership with his powerful and riveting book, Connect the Dots. *Not only does Dick clearly spell out the key principles for attaining and sustaining success in today's "Now" economy, but he has ingeniously done so with illustrations from real leaders who have already proven his theories. A must-read for anyone on the path to leadership!*

—Darcel Harris Butler, president and CEO, Lessons in Learning, Inc.

Insightful and passionate. I thoroughly enjoyed reading Connect the Dots. *I recommend* Connect the Dots *and its framework to anyone who wants to be an IMPACT Player!*

—Timothy Tuttle, CFO, Intelligent Decision Solutions

Take the time to read Connect the Dots *and what has been discovered and elegantly shared here. More important, take the time to personally reflect on the wisdom in these everyday lessons. You will enjoy your individual return on investment! I know that my personal network of dots will be getting a copy from me to enrich our connections.*

—Bill Hitchcock, solution delivery executive, EDS

Connect the Dots *is inspiration. Discovering one's Impact Niche is essential to a successful career as well as a life brimming with significance. Realizing the fullness of your personal potential is the key to life success.*

—Robin Wood, president, Authentic Living

Connect the Dots *is an excellent and practical book for anyone in business. Dick Lynch's concepts are right on! And hearing about their application by people who live them is profoundly effective! Bravo! Well done!*

—John Feloni, CEO, StockbrokerPro.com, and co-author of
The Fall of the House of Hutton (Henry Holt, 1988)

Connect the Dots *is a worthy read for individuals who understand, or wish to understand, the difference between interest and commitment. The path outlined in* Connect the Dots *embodies the philosophy of "hard to do, but easy to live with" that can lead to fulfillment and success in all of life's endeavors.*

—Tim Dolan, private investor

Dick Lynch has done a fantastic job of pulling together some of the greatest philosophies of progress and success available. Connect the Dots *is a "how to" book for anyone seeking success.*

—Joe Maas, vice president, JTM Food Group

In Connect the Dots, *Dick Lynch outlines methods that individuals, organizations, and communities use to establish high performance and resiliency. It's a must-read for people interested in building success.*

—Matt Paknis, Paknis Consulting

Connect the Dots...To Become An Impact Player

Dick Lynch

Founder of the Impact Player League &
the Impact Player Institute

iUniverse, Inc.
New York Lincoln Shanghai

Connect the Dots...To Become An Impact Player

iUniverse, Inc.

For information address:
iUniverse
2021 Pine Lake Road, Suite 100
Lincoln, NE 68512
www.iuniverse.com

ISBN: 0-595-29492-8 (Pbk)
ISBN: 0-595-75008-7 (Cloth)

Printed in the United States of America

This book is dedicated to my lovely wife, Karen, and my four wonderful children, Ryan, Grant, Claire, and Ethan. I love you so! Also to Mom, Claire Ann Lynch, a beautiful person.

In Honor

This book is also a small attempt to honor the heroes of September 11th, especially Todd Beamer* (Flight 93). I never met this special person, but his inspiration is with me every day. Also: my ever-smiling friend and Brown University football teammate Dave Laycheck, who gave his life for our country at the Pentagon. The kindest person I ever knew.

Never in the field of human conflict was so much owed by so many to so few.

—Winston Churchill

The author will make a donation to the United Negro College Fund and The Todd M. Beamer Foundation from part of his proceeds of the book.

* The Todd M. Beamer Foundation is a non-profit public charity created to enable children experiencing family trauma to make heroic choices every day. In honor of Todd Beamer and the other heroes of United Flight 93, Todd's family and friends established The Foundation to carry on his legacy of character, faith, and courage to a new generation of young people.

If this book has made a difference in your life, please consider making a donation to The Todd M. Beamer Foundation at www.beamerfoundation.org and/or the United Negro College Fund at www.uncf.org. Thank you.

Contents

Foreword by Dr. Kevin Elko xv

Introduction 1
    Reggie Williams 5

Glossary 9

Part 1   Education

Dot #1 15
    Howard Stevens 19
    Christian Okoye 23

Dot # 2 27
    Richard Cavanagh 29
    Bruce Rector 31
    William Mundell 35

Dot #3 37
    Brendan Foley 39

The Impact Player Challenge 43

The HR Chally Group 49

Part 2   Inspiration

Impact Players and Their Inspirational Interviews 53
    Diane Swonk 55
    Dick Traum 59
    Governor Martha Layne Collins 63
    Neil Bush 67
    Fred Scrutchfield 73
    Rick Novak 77
    Ed Rigaud 81
    Doug MacMillan 87

Sally Stewart 91
Pat Manocchia 95
Dr. Kevin Elko 99
Dick Wilson 103
Brendan McPhillips 105

LEADERSHIP—Lessons in Leadership 107

IMPACT LEADERS—How Impact Players Lead 113
Coach Marvin Lewis 115
Dr. Lee Todd 119
Bill Robinson 125

Building an Impact Player Organization 127

The Impact Leader Challenge 133

The Impact Player Awards 135

Part 3   Innovation

Corporate Innovation 139
A. G. Lafley 141
Joe Stimac 145
Dr. James Canton 149
Dick Lajoie 153
Bob Messenger 157

Brand Innovation 159
Andrew Arken 161

Regional Innovation 167
Dr. Ralph Snyderman 169
Dr. William Brundage 173
Dr. Stuart Rosenfeld 177

Entrepreneurial Innovation 181
Earvin "Magic" Johnson 181
Dr. Jeffry Timmons 183

Demographic Shifts & Innovation 185
Gary Wright 187

Women in Business 189
Dr. Dotty Heady 193

The Impact Society & Diversity 197
    Eric Hoyt 199
Developing an Innovation Culture 205
    Kris Kimel & Joanne Lang 211

Part 4   Aggregation
The Impact Player League 215

Afterword 221
    Your Legacy Starts Today 221
    Predictions for the Impact Society 222

Appendix 225
    Impact Player Assessment Example 226
    Impact Leader Assessment Example 230
    Recommended Reading for Impact Players 234

ILLUSTRATIONS: Connect the Dots Illustrations 237

About the Author 255

Foreword by Dr. Kevin Elko

Have you ever sat in front of any empty bowl and thought, How did the ice cream that was in the bowl a minute ago disappear? Most of us have had that experience, of course. The reason is we were not in a fully conscious state as we ate—at least, we weren't conscious of eating. Research studies have concluded that one of the best ways to lose weight, a topic on most minds these days, is simply to write down everything you eat. What that does is awaken you to what you're putting in your mouth.

Dick Lynch's book is so valuable because he wrote down the inspirational and educational no-nonsense advice of successful people, awakening us to what we, as human beings, should be doing with our lives.

He wrote this exceptional book to help awaken us to new realities. There are powerful interviews with leaders to help people, businesses, organizations, and even cities with their awakening. He calls these leading individuals that positively shape their world Impact Players. The focus of these Impact Players is on Continuous Performance Improvement. Impact Players passionately and consistently try to improve themselves and everyone with whom they come into contact.

Heed the words of these Impact Players. People who do so will build successful careers. Businesses that do so will create new products and loyal customers. Organizations that do so will fulfill their purposes in new, creative ways. Cities that do so will foster an environment of wealth creation and prosperity.

Listen to Diane Swonk, chief economist for Bank One and a survivor of the World Trade Center attack, when she says all of us have something to learn. "If one theme should resonate from September 11th, it is that the lives of our children are desperately dependent upon how children around the world view their own fates."

Listen to A. G. Lafley, chairman and CEO of Procter & Gamble, when he says, "Businesses that resist change will not survive. Those that adapt to change may survive, but they will not lead. Those that shape change, that turn it to their advantage and grow as a result of it, not in spite of it, win—often disproportionately."

Listen to Dr. William Brundage, commissioner of the Office for the New Economy in the Commonwealth of Kentucky, when he says, "Building the infrastructure for the knowledge-based economy is a team sport. It requires the collaboration of business, government, and academia and a blurring of the lines that separate their roles."

The solution for a successful life is to wake up and become an Impact Player. In *Connect The Dots...To Become an Impact Player*, Dick Lynch helps you discover how to do something important: Wake up and reach your potential.

Vision is a vital part of any awakened life. Fulfilling a vision, or failing to do so, is directly related to discipline, passion, and process. What this book does so well is highlight the discipline, passion, and processes that real people in real situations use for Continuous Performance Improvement.

While reading this unique book, pay attention to "you speaking to you." Become conscious of the inner conversations it prompts you to have. Then be intelligent about what "you start to say to you." Instead of saying, "I have to cope with my job today," say, "I am going to become an Impact Player and win today."

Finally, take to heart the words of Dick Traum, who was the first leg amputee to finish a marathon. "When you are disabled," Dick says, "you learn very quickly that we are all brothers and sisters on this planet. Race, religion, gender, political orientation, and ethnicity all evaporate in the shared experiences of the disabled."

I heartily suggest that you keep *Connect the Dots...To Become an Impact Player* close to you at all times and use it as your guidebook to your new awakening as an Impact Player.

—Dr. Kevin Elko

Dr. Kevin Elko, a psychologist, has consulted with and made presentations to many of the nation's top companies, including Travelers Insurance, The Young Presidents Organization, Smith Kline Beecham Consumer Brands, Abbott Diagnostics, Prudential Securities, Salomon Smith Barney, Merrill Lynch, University of Pittsburgh Athletic Department, University of Miami Football, The Pittsburgh Penguins, The Dallas Cowboys, The New Orleans Saints, The Cleveland Browns, The Miami Dolphins, The Philadelphia Eagles, Pioneer Investments, and The Israel Wingate Institute.

Dr. Elko completed his bachelor's degree in Biology and Coaching Education at California University of Pennsylvania. At Virginia University, he completed a master's in Counseling, a master's in Sports Psychology, a graduate certificate in Gerontology and a doctorate in Education with a major emphasis on Sports and Counseling. He is a certified addictions counselor.

Acknowledgements

My sincere appreciation goes to:

all the wonderful leaders that taught me so much in these terrific interviews;

Gwen Flanders, for her superb editorial talents;

Brian Krueger and Tom Shingleton, for their artistic prowess on the cover and the *Connect the Dot* illustrations;

Dr. Rob Snyder, Darcel Harris, Chris Schearer, Bill Robinson, Rich Hempel, and Ed Walton, for their suggestions on how to make this book a better read;

Dr. Bill Brundage, a visionary who has helped me pursue my dreams;

and my father, Hank Lynch, the biggest Impact Player in my life.

Thank you all!

Introduction

We were born to succeed, not to fail.

—Henry David Thoreau, philosopher

How to Make This Book Work for You

If you are passionate about results for yourself and your organization, then read this book. I would like to make one thing clear right from the beginning: In this book I will not tell you how to get the most out of life. Rather, I will introduce you to some of the greatest Impact Players in the world, giving you their perspective on how to achieve success. One of the first things you'll notice is that I broadened the use of the term Impact Player, which has been used almost exclusively in sports, and applied it to positive leaders across all of society. This book distills the ideas of these Impact Players into a clear plan you can follow. I simply *Connected the Dots* (their messages) on what it takes to be an Impact Player.

The book is divided into the four parts (dots) that when connected form a clear picture of an Impact Player: Education, Inspiration, Innovation, and Aggregation.

Part 1: Education clearly defines what you need to know to become an Impact Player. This section also offers you a challenge to do so.
Part 2: Inspiration contains Impact Player interviews that will inspire you to do things right and do the right things.
Part 3: Innovation provides expert advice on why cities, businesses, and all organizations must embrace diversity and change and have exceptional leadership to survive.
Part 4: Aggregation illustrates how every person, race, and culture are in this game of life together and why we must develop a fellowship of diversity for our children and ourselves. In this section you'll discover the Impact Player League.

The one common denominator in all of these parts is what I call Continuous Performance Improvement (CPI). I define CPI as the relentless, constant, and never-ending pursuit of excellence that Impact Players (individuals and organizations) undertake in their quest to be the best.

1

This book contains powerful interviews with Impact Players. Reggie Williams' thoughts are a tremendous primer on what awaits you in the rest of *Connect the Dots...To Become an Impact Player*.

Reggie Williams

Reggie Williams—passionate about the game of life

I can't imagine a person becoming a success who doesn't give this game of life everything he's got.

—Walter Cronkite, legendary CBS anchor

When you meet Reggie Williams, one word captures the essence of his being: PASSION. Reggie Williams is the most passionate man I have ever met. He believes that passion is the key for Continuous Performance Improvement.

During his sports career, Reggie received honors that included:

➢ NFL All-Rookie Team (1976)

➢ The Byron "Whizzer" White Award for Humanitarian Service (1985)

➢ NFL Man of the Year (1986)

➢ Sports Illustrated's Co-Sportsman of the Year (1987)

➢ Two Super Bowl Appearances, XVI (1982) and XXIII (1989)

➢ Ivy League heavyweight wrestling champion at Dartmouth College (1975)

➢ Three-time All-Ivy League linebacker.

Why is Reggie Williams an Impact Player? Passion. "Passion is at the very heart of success," he says. "Passion is an insatiable love that can't be satisfied. And passionate people are great to be around. Passion must be recognized as a source of strength. Athletes must be passionate about playing sports. Business people must be passionate about selling their product. Politicians must be passionate about moving public opinion.

"Passion is the most transferable of all personality traits. Passion is a magnetic quality. Passion is about being a champion. Passion is intrinsic, but it can be taught. Passion is always sincere. That's why passion is the authentic real deal! Passion holds the Impact Players on your team together. Passion to embrace innovation and change brings about growth and success. Passion makes people say, "Bring it on!" when they face a steep challenge or the trials and tribulations of life.

"Passion is at the core of being a disciplined person. Did I like conditioning drills, or running stadium steps, or doing those last reps with weights? No. But I was passionate about giving those kids that came to the games on Sunday the best game I could. Why? Because I knew they were living vicariously through me. As a child, I lived through Jim Brown, Gayle Sayers, and Willie Lanier. As a professional football player, I had a responsibility to every child in that stadium to be the best that I could be.

"And now my childhood dreams are responsible for my career opportunities. Now it is my responsibility to be passionate about my work at Walt Disney World and make every child that comes here have memories of this place being the happiest place on Earth. After all, everyone must be passionate about kids, about their dreams, and about the journey that we're all on together. Everyone must be passionate about becoming an Impact Player in the game of life."

Currently, as vice president of sports and recreation for the Walt Disney Company, Reggie is focused on creating exhilarating guest and cast experiences for those who work and play at Disney's sports and recreation facilities. Reggie is responsible for Disney's water parks, two miniature golf courses, ninety-nine holes of golf, resort recreation, and Disney's Wide World of Sports Complex, as well as their operating participant, Walt Disney World Speedway. Reggie oversees sports development and management, sales and marketing, budget and strategy, sports industry relations, and new product development, as well as merchandise strategy and operations for the business unit as a whole.

Here are a few suggestions on how to make the best use of this book:

1) Skip around. After you've read the introduction and brief glossary, you can open the book to any page and learn something.

2) Once you've reviewed the ideas, examples, and suggestions of this book, make them your own. Incorporate them into your life. The combination of interviews, short essays, and connect-the-dot illustrations is a powerful delivery mechanism.

3) Take this book when you travel. It's a quick read.

4) Keep it close to you. If you have a problem making a business decision, there is enough practical advice here to clear your head and point you in the right direction.

5) When you read this book, think about time, our most valuable asset. Your time to become an Impact Player in the world is not tomorrow, not soon—it's now!

6) As you read, make notes to yourself. All the wisdom isn't written here. It's also in you, and this book can help you make the most of it. Use a marker to highlight those sections or ideas that mean the most to you, because those are the sections that have the greatest potential for impacting your life.

Writing This Book Was the Opportunity of a Lifetime

It was exciting to interview, listen to, and learn from such a wide array of successful people. The experience was humbling, and I appreciate the time and gifts of insight that the participants generously shared.

Listen and Learn to Connect the Dots

For more than two years, I traveled the country to listen to and/or meet with some of the greatest practitioners of Continuous Performance Improvement in the world. These Impact Players included President George W. Bush, Jack Welch, Earvin "Magic" Johnson, Mayor Rudy Giuliani, James Baker, Vice President Dick Cheney, Sharon Allen, Joaquin Blaya, Steve Forbes, Larry King, Terrence Lanni, Suzanne Nora Johnson, and Stephen Covey.

To further *Connect the Dots*, I and other senior executives founded The Leadership Club and the Impact Player Institute. To improve our knowledge, we widened our network of Impact Players to learn from Vicky Jones, director of leadership at General Motors; Neil Bush, education visionary and proud member of our nation's first family; Dr. Bill Brundage, top authority to United States governors on innovation and commercialization; Reggie Williams, senior executive at Disney and Sports Illustrated Sportsman of the Year; Congressman Ken Lucas, who represents Kentucky in the U.S. House of Representatives; Doug MacMillan, CEO of The Todd M. Beamer Foundation; Christian Okoye, all-pro with the Kansas City Chiefs and American success story from Nigeria; Eric Hoyt, foremost expert on business development for the Hispanic and Latino marketplace; the Honorable J. Kenneth Blackwell, Ohio's Secretary of State; and Bruce Rector, president of the 200,000-member entrepreneurial organization Junior Chamber International.

Finally, we collected even more data points on what it takes to achieve Continuous Performance Improvement by interviewing more Impact Players, including: A. G. Lafley, chairman and CEO, Procter & Gamble; Diane Swonk, chief economist and senior vice president at Bank One and author of *The Passionate Economist*; Ed Rigaud, president of the National Underground Railroad Freedom Center; Bill Mundell, CEO of Vidyah; Richard Cavanagh, president & CEO of The Conference Board; Sally Stewart, author of *Media Training 101*, former chief West Coast correspondent for *USA TODAY*; Marvin Lewis, head coach of the Cincinnati Bengals; Kris Kimel and Joanne Lang, founders of the ideaFestival; Dr. Jeffry Timmons, renowned entrepreneurial expert, Babson College; Dr. Jim Votruba, president of Northern Kentucky University; Pat Manocchia, CEO of La Palestra and former national fitness expert on *Good Morning America*; Bob Messenger, trend guru in the food-and-beverage industry; Dick Traum, founder of the Achilles Track Club; Eddy Roberts, president of BellSouth Kentucky; Gary Wright, associate director of the Global Trends Group at Procter & Gamble; Nigel Oxbrow, international authority on knowledge management and innovation ; Jay McChord, Generation-X bridge-builder; Dr. Dotty Heady, entrepreneur and leadership instructor at Sullivan University's International Center for Dispute Resolution & Leadership; Joe Stimac, developer of the Innovation Algorithm; Kurt Mueller, senior executive with the Ewing Marion Kauffman Foundation; William Robinson, member of the Board of Governors and chair of the finance committee of the American Bar Association; Dr. Lee Todd, president of the University of Kentucky; Howard Stevens, CEO of The HR Chally Group; Dr. James Canton, founder and CEO, Institute for Global Futures; Dick Wilson, senior vice president for investments; Dr. Stuart Rosenfeld, founder and CEO, RTS, Inc.; Dr. Kevin Elko, renowned sports and business psychologist; Dick Lajoie, CFO, Belcan Corp.; Governor Martha Layne Collins, executive in residence at Georgetown College; and Dr. Ralph Snyderman, president and CEO of the Duke University Health System and chair of the American Association of Medical Colleges.

Glossary

Continuous Performance Improvement (CPI)

CPI is the relentless, constant, and never-ending pursuit of excellence that Impact Players (individuals and organizations) undertake in their quest to be the best.

Impact Niche

An Impact Niche is the skill set you possess that provides uniqueness and value to society and which results in wealth creation for you.

Impact Players

Impact Players combine their natural talent with the motivation needed to use that talent in a consistent and predictable fashion to produce superior results.

As individuals they are mobile, well-educated professionals who thrive on performance and results. Impact Players can be executives, frontline workers, salespersons, nurses, doctors, lawyers, software engineers, medical technicians, scientists, entertainers, politicians, professors, athletes, writers, or entrepreneurs.

Because communications tools are inexpensive, Impact Players can live almost anywhere. Impact Players continually update their skills with job experience and adapt to change before they have to. Most important, Impact Players focus on results and have the passion and energy to execute plans. And just like Impact Players in sports, Impact Players in business, government, academia, not-for-profit organizations, and entertainment are highly mobile and command a great deal of money in the marketplace. Impact Players are shaping the next economy—the "Impact Economy"™—where you have to focus on results because the competition is intense.

Impact Players have:

1) Talent necessary for the job.
2) Motivation to excel.

3) High energy to execute a plan.

4) Vision to know where they're going.

5) Self-discipline to work long hours.

6) Persistence to overcome obstacles.

7) Burning passion for diversity and innovation.

8) Commitment to serve others.

9) Emotional intensity that positively impacts others.

10) Correct self-assessment of their skills, which allows them to set goals that are specific, attainable, measurable, reviewable, and trackable.

Impact Leaders

Impact Leaders are individuals who are responsible for an organization of Impact Players.

Impact Leaders:

1) Understand, appreciate, empower, and serve people, which motivates them to achieve their clearly-articulated organizational focus of positively shaping the individual, organization, and society.

2) Are passionate reality visionaries.

3) Thrive on being an innovator and an agent of change.

4) Listen to a diverse group of individuals supplying a broader perspective, which enables them to make more well-informed decisions.

5) Communicate their vision clearly, consistently, and constantly.

6) Know what the strengths and motivations (Impact Niche) are for each Impact Player in the organization.

7) Play to the strengths of each Impact Player on the team.

8) Lead Impact Players and don't manage them.

9) Focus on winning.

10) Break the business year into seasons.

Impact Player Awards

The Impact Player Awards honor people and organizations that excel at embracing change, diversity, innovation, and service to others while achieving unparalleled success in their field of expertise. The Impact Player Awards are the first awards that recognize individuals and organizations that are positively impacting the many stakeholders of society.

Impact Player Challenge (IPC)

IPC is a step-by-step program that enables people to become the best they can be. People who are successful in the Impact Player Challenge understand their strengths and motivations and wrap their careers around those strengths and motivations.

The Impact Leader Challenge (ILC)

ILC is a step-by-step program that provides executives, responsible for the effectiveness of people and organizations, with a template to help them maximize the productivity of each player on the team.

Impact Player League (IPL)

IPL is an organization that focuses on building relationships among leaders from all walks of life based on healthy competition and shared experiences.

Impact Economy

The Impact Economy is today's hyper-competitive economy. It is an economy that rewards only those people responsible for making unique and value-oriented offerings to the end user.

Impact Society

The Impact Society describes the new demands of society today and for the immediate future. In this society, embracing diversity and service to all stakeholders is a prerequisite for success.

Part 1

Education

Become an Impact Player: The Three Dots

Always bear in mind that your own resolution to success is more important than any other one thing.

—Abraham Lincoln

Connect the Dots...To Become an Impact Player™

As children, we played *Connect the Dots* for fun. The dots provided us with direction, a roadmap on where to go next to draw a picture. The outline of a tree, an elephant, or a flower quickly came into view with a few strokes of a pencil. Connecting the dots made it possible to outline a clear picture of something that normally we couldn't have drawn without the alignment of the dots.

Now we're adults. It's time to connect the dots again, not for fun, but for our economic survival and personal development. Again, the dots provide us with direction, a roadmap on how to become an Impact Player.

Connect the Dots helps us discover how Impact Players overcome the two big C's of life: Change & Challenge.

Connect the Dots... To Become an Impact Player provides corporate executives, business professionals, city planners, politicians, academic leaders, small business owners and entrepreneurs with a clear picture on how to reach one's full potential.

The Three Dots That Form the Picture of an Impact Player:

1.   Build a career around your strengths and motivations.
2.   Develop a vision and a diverse network to help execute that vision.
3.   Embrace change and innovation to better serve stakeholders.

Continuous Performance Improvement is a major part of all three dots.

Dot #1: Become an Impact Player by Building a Career around Your Strengths and Motivations

Know thyself.

—Plato

Knowing and understanding oneself is a prerequisite for becoming an Impact Player and the first step on the Continuous Performance Improvement Journey—a journey that never ends.

Impact Player Defined

Impact Players combine one's natural talent with the motivation needed to use that talent in a consistent and predictable fashion to produce superior results.

"Impact Players" are a mobile group of well-educated professionals who thrive on performance and results. Impact Players can be executives, craftsmen, salespersons, nurses, doctors, frontline service people, lawyers, software engineers, medical technicians, scientists, entertainers, politicians, professors, athletes, writers, or entrepreneurs.

They can reside anywhere in the world. Anyone can do business anywhere in the world because of the Internet's connectivity. Because of the Internet, many white-collar jobs are moving abroad. To be competitive, Impact Players in the United States and all nations must continue to focus on the following tenets.

Impact Players are people who have:

1) Talent necessary for their job.

2) Motivation to excel at their work.

3) High energy to execute their plan.

4) Vision to know where they're going.

5) Self-discipline to work long hours.

6) Persistence to overcome obstacles.

7) Burning passion for diversity and innovation.

8)   Commitment to serve others.

9)   Emotional intensity that positively impacts others.

10) Correct self-assessment of their skills, which allows them to set goals that are specific, attainable, measurable, flexible, reviewable, and trackable.

> *"A successful individual typically sets his next goal somewhat but not too much above his last achievement. In this way he steadily raises his level of aspiration."*
>
> **—Kurt Lewin, pioneering behavioral psychologist**

An Impact Player Must Focus On His or Her Impact Niche

To be truly successful, you need to understand your business talents and develop a career around those strengths and motivations. We call people who do this Impact Players. We call your skill-set your *Impact Niche.*

To reiterate, an Impact Player combines natural talent with the motivation to use that talent in a consistent and predictable way to produce superior results.

> *What is the recipe for successful achievement? To my mind there are just four essential ingredients: Choose a career you love, give it the best there is in you, seize your opportunities, and be a member of the team.*
>
> **—Benjamin F. Fairless, former president, U.S. Steel**

Howard Stevens

Howard Stevens, CEO of The HR Chally Group, a professional assessment organization, uses a baseball analogy to describe the Impact Niche phenomenon. On a T-ball team, kids who can swing a bat and not fall down are good enough to make the team. On a high school team, kids have to be able to throw, run, catch, and hit. They have to be total athletes.

But when you get to the pros, being a total athlete is merely the price of admission. Each of these players concentrates on developing one or two strengths—their Impact Niche.

This specialization, the Impact Niche, gets them to the big leagues and keeps them there. Professional baseball managers look for the very best pitchers, outfielders, and infielders. Professional players usually excel at one or, at most, two skills. People with well-defined Impact Niches in baseball include Roger Clemens, who is a strikeout artist; Hank Aaron, who specialized in home runs; and Ozzie Smith, who could make spectacular plays in the infield. Pitchers usually can't hit well, infielders rarely excel in the outfield, and it would be a story in the newspaper if anyone but a pitcher pitched. Professional players, at the highest levels of performance, focus and work on their strengths because that Impact Niche produces the most value for the team.

Impact Niche in Business

Do not let what you cannot do interfere with what you can do.
—John Wooden, unequaled UCLA basketball coach

The same holds true for people in business. Someone who understands what his or her Impact Niche is and builds a career around their strengths is well on the way to way to becoming successful. Different people possess different business talents. Diane Swonk is an analyzer and synthesizer, Bill Gates is an innovator, Earvin "Magic" Johnson is an entrepreneur, and Jack Welch excels at choosing leaders to run lines of business. Different positions in an organization, such as sales, management, and operations, require different skill sets.

Business today has a great deal in common with professional sports. Individuals and companies must understand and play to their strengths. Don't focus on what you can't do; focus on what you can do. The more intense the competition, the more important it is to have people who focus on the Impact Niche. That is as true for businesses as it is for individuals. Both must focus and play to their Impact Niche. When you focus on your Impact Niche, you are on your way to becoming an Impact Player.

Impact Players™

Act as if what you do makes a difference. It does.
—William James, psychologist and philosopher

We hear and read about Impact Players in sports all the time. At a minimum, they have unwavering competitiveness. Impact Players deliver in clutch situations and are positive spirits. They are intelligent and prepared for their defining moment, and they live to make the big play. Impact Players often overcome overwhelming odds and personal tragedies only to soar when their team needs them the most. But most of all, Impact Players are *passionate*. They leave a positive emotional imprint on teammates and opponents alike, an imprint that makes everyone they meet try a little harder in life.

You are not here merely to make a living. You are here in order to enable the world to live more amply, with greater vision, with a finer spirit of hope and achievement.

—Woodrow Wilson

Impact Player Mobility

Impact Players continually update their skills with job experience, and they adapt to change before they have to. Most importantly, Impact Players focus on results and have the passion and energy to execute their plans. And just like Impact Players in sports, Impact Players in society are highly mobile—today's inexpensive communication tools make it possible for them to live almost anywhere—and command a great deal of money in the marketplace. Impact Players are shaping the next economy, the Impact Economy, where the intensity of the competition means they have to focus on results.

Impact Players are by nature: talented, passionate, innovative, results-driven, motivated and appreciative of diversity. Impact Players are Continuous Performance Improvement junkies.

Impact Players in the U.S. Military

To get a clear picture of the productivity and efficiency of Impact Players, look at our military's Special Forces. Special Force personnel are Impact Players. They are specialists trained in the latest technologies, they do their job with little or no supervision at the point of engagement, and they are responsible for a major objective today: winning the War against Terrorism. Our military Impact Players undergo exhaustive formal training and even more training in the field. The training meshes with a well-thought-out plan, developed with an organizational focus that makes it clear how their work fits into the big picture.

Christian Okoye

Christian Okoye

Your work is to discover your world and then with all your heart give your-self to it.

—**Buddha**

Connect the Dots and you'll notice that Impact Players have a can-do and will-do attitude. They have the talent to do the job—that's the can-do part. And they have the motivation to excel—that's the will-do part. Impact Players excel in whatever they undertake. That's because they are continually looking at ways to improve themselves.

One of the greatest Impact Players I have ever had the privilege of getting to know is Christian Okoye, the former All-Pro running back with the Kansas City Chiefs. Everybody should have the opportunity to meet this man, because he is a priceless original. While I was playing golf with him one day in Kansas City, four very distinguished-looking senior women ran across two fairways to get his autograph and say hello. They talked and hugged Christian like he was a long-lost sibling. This happens everywhere he goes. Missouri, Ohio, Arizona, Kentucky, or California—it doesn't matter. He is bigger than life but gentler than a child. Yet the firmness of his resolve is clearly evident. He's here to excel in business and help those less fortunate to be positive participants in society. Christian Okoye is a difference-maker in the lives of people. He is an Impact Player.

His story

Christian Okoye was born in Enugu, Nigeria. He had a very loving and supportive mother and father. Even though his family was very poor, his parents always managed to provide Christian and his three brothers and three sisters with essentials, such as shoes. As a kid, Christian played soccer, not football. To this day, soccer is his sport of choice. Given the choice between a good game of soccer and a good game of football, Christian will watch soccer every time.

In the early 1980s, Christian had a friend who attended Azusa Pacific University. That friend told the track-and-field coach at Azusa Pacific about an athlete back in Nigeria who excelled in the discus and the shot put. At twenty-one years of age, Christian Okoye received a scholarship to attend Azusa Pacific. It would be his first experience away from Nigeria. When he got to the United States, he didn't know what to think. He was in awe of the stability of America. That isn't surprising considering that Christian spent his youth in the midst of a civil war.

Christian wasn't just good in track and field; he was a world-class athlete. He won seven national titles in shot put, discus, and the hammer and won All-American honors in track and field. While at Azusa Pacific, he trained to throw the discus and shot put for Nigeria in the Olympics. But for some reason, Christian was left off of the Nigerian Olympic Team. He thinks it was politics, but to this day, he doesn't know why he was left off the team.

Angry, frustrated, and disappointed, he focused his energies on a new sport, football. Christian excelled right away at football, but he had to overcome a major hurdle: he didn't like the contact. He didn't like it all. At six foot, two inches and 260 pounds, an aversion to contact may seem odd. But Christian grew up with the finesse of soccer, not the contact of football. (This illustrates the importance of understanding the orientation of others.) Christian even thought of quitting, but he had exceptional support and encouragement from his friends. Besides, if he made it to the National Football League, he could send money home to his family back in Nigeria.

In 1987, the Kansas City Chiefs drafted Christian Okoye in the second round of the NFL Draft. Christian went on to have a stellar professional football career. His outstanding 1989 season culminated in an array of awards, including Running Back of the Year and first team All-Pro. The National Football League Players Association voted Christian the American Football Conference's Most Valuable Player, and he received the Mackie award for most touchdowns in the AFC. Christian got MVP honors from the Kansas City Chiefs, and the Quarterback Club of Washington, D.C., named him the league MVP. He credits his Impact Player status in football to his will to succeed as well as his talent. What also drove Christian to become an Impact Player was his fear of failure. He didn't want to let himself or those around him down.

Christian has taken those same strengths and become an Impact Player in business and society. In business, he owns his own line of health-care products, called Okoye Fitness (www.okoyefitness.com). His fitness and nutrition company offers scientifically-advanced nutritional products designed to facilitate weight loss and weight management and to promote better health in general. When I asked him who had done his web site, he proudly proclaimed, "Me!" He credits superior business people like Lamar Hunt, founder of the American Football Conference and the Kansas City Chiefs, and Carl Peterson, the Chiefs' CEO, with teaching him how to be a successful entrepreneur. He also helped himself by attending conferences, trade shows, and workshops.

However, what Christian is most passionate about is helping kids. Not just one or two, but thousands of children every year in Los Angeles, Kansas City, and throughout the country. Every year, he arranges the donation of over 20,000 stuffed animals to children's hospitals. Christian also holds sports camps for troubled kids. Knowing how kids respond well to athletes, he invited many of his old playing buddies to join him.

Mixed in with lessons on football are the lessons of life. He brings in a nutritionist, and he talks about staying in school and staying away from drugs. He's been putting on these camps since 1990, and he finances them through his own fundraising, receiving no government support. If he's short on funds he kicks in his own money. Men who were boys at his camps twelve years ago still stop by to thank Christian for being there. They visit with their wives and kids and with successful careers in front of them. Christian provided them with a positive influence instead of the negative influences they saw every day. One person can make a difference!

But Christian doesn't have to wait twelve years to see the payoff of his investment in the community. Kids who arrive with a chip on their shoulder usually leave his camp with a smile. When I asked Christian how those handshakes and smiles made him feel, he said, "Warm all over, man." These smiles make him feel better than any touchdown he ever scored. Christian Okoye is the epitome of an Impact Player.

Christian Okoye's Impact Niche

Christian Okoye knows his strengths. He is an expert in health and nutrition and a man that knows his motivators. For example, helping people motivates him. Logically, then, he has developed a career around his strengths and motivation. His business, Okoye Fitness, helps people become healthier and happier through exercise and diet. Christian is especially motivated to help children. He enhances his success in life by running fitness and sports camps for disadvantaged children. Christian is an Impact Player because his career revolves around his strengths and motivations.

Dot # 2: Have a Vision and Develop a Diverse Network of Impact Players to Help You Execute That Vision.

The path to greatness is along with others.
—Baltasar Gracion, seventeenth-century Spanish Priest

Richard Cavanagh

The Importance of Vision and a Diverse Network

Everything starts with a vision. Webster defines vision as "unusual discernment or foresight." Impact Players have vision. The leaders I interviewed and listened to say a vision is usually the result of a synthesis of experiences.

Virtually every Impact Player stressed the importance of having a diverse network of Impact Players to help you develop your vision. When you surround yourself and compete with people who are the best, it pushes you to become the best. A good network of leaders guides you to develop your vision. And when you're looking for a business partner, a confidant, good advice, or just a friend to talk to, your network of Impact Players becomes invaluable. Surround yourself with a diverse team of Impact Players to hone your Continuous Performance Improvement.

One of the most important tenets of the Impact Society is having an extensive network of Impact Players. Why? Because Impact Players possess a wealth of knowledge and information, and they thrive on helping others. According to Dick Cavanagh, CEO and president of The Conference Board, his organization's members had a 95% renewal rate during last year's recession. Why? Because Impact Players know the importance of staying connected, and they wisely spent their money on a Conference Board membership. The Conference Board has an exceptional network of executives.

Go Outside Your Organization

Nobody ever came up with a great idea all by themselves.

—Thomas Edison

Impact Players develop their network with other Impact Players outside their industry. This exposure helps businesses borrow ideas from other kinds of businesses. Dick Cavanagh has seen it happen all the time. If lifetime warranties are effective for knives, why not pens? If luxury cars can be sold on value, why not chicken?

Impact Players understand that a personal and professional network of Impact Players is one of the most valuable assets you can have. Impact Players take time out to meet other Impact Players and establish relationships with them. Impact Players join organizations that place them in the company of other Impact Players.

Bruce Rector

International Network

A network of international contacts is important because Impact Players with great ideas exist in all nations. Bruce Rector, president of Junior Chamber International (JCI), knows this fact and is acting upon it. JCI has more than 200,000 members from 110 countries and territories. Bruce will be visiting more than sixty countries this year alone! He is building a tremendous network of Impact Players. Please read about this exciting organization at www.jci.cc.

Build Your Network by Providing Value to Others First

The key to developing a powerful Impact Player network is to do things for other people first without expecting anything in return. Help people you meet succeed and you will reap success yourself. When you meet an Impact Player, always do something for him or her first. Impact Players help everyone around them succeed, especially those less fortunate. As Stephen Covey, author of *The 7 Habits of Highly Effective People*, wisely says, true leaders always try to understand others before they expect to be understood. Impact Players listen and promote the cause of other Impact Players. They build their network by introducing Impact Players to other Impact Players. It takes time to build an Impact Player network, but the process is rewarding!

Start building it now. Join a leadership association. Do something for other Impact Players without expecting anything in return. One caveat: Make sure that the people you are associating with are Impact Players and not dreamers. How do you tell the difference? Look around at the people with whom they associate.

A Diverse Network Is Key

> *Civilizations should be measured by the degree of diversity attained and the degree of unity retained.*
>
> —W. H. Auden, poet

Make your Impact Player network as diverse as possible. You gain a better understanding of the real world when you surround yourself with Impact Players of different backgrounds, races, religions, and experiences.

The active exchange of ideas among a diverse group of Impact Players must be facilitated at conferences and seminars, via email and over the phone. *It is imperative to meet them in person on a regular basis.* The excuse of being too busy just doesn't cut it. There is something special and effective about personal contact. It cannot be replaced by any other communication. Impact Players who establish symbiotic relationships with other Impact Players in a diverse group will thrive. These people are the innovators, and they are shaping the Impact Economy.

The key benefit of diversity is the insight you get from listening to people who have different perspectives. Diversity helps both people and organizations grow.

Diverse perspectives foster new insights. New insights result in novelty. Novelty results in the development of new products and services. The commercialization of novel ideas leads to profits. Organizations that promote diversity are always evolving. Diverse organizations that embrace change and innovation are more apt to survive. An individual with a diverse circle of Impact Players has an enhanced orientation and is a better businessperson because of it.

William Mundell

William Mundell

A business and personal network is vital to success today. "Diverse input" allows successful people to make better, more well-informed decisions while executing their vision. The reach of a person's network should be global. This statement is especially true for Impact Leaders. (Impact Players in positions of leadership are Impact Leaders.) An international network is especially important if an Impact Leader is trying to maximize the growth of an organization. Impact Leaders are passionate "reality" visionaries, innovators, and change agents who listen to a diverse group of individuals within their formal and informal business network.

People do not change with the times. They change the times.

—P.K. Shaw

Bill Mundell's Impact Niche is his unparalleled knowledge of international trade combined with a business network that is second to none. Helping organizations solve problems and providing a high return for his shareholders are two of Bill's motivators. His Impact Niche of international trade and his international network of business executives have enabled Bill to develop a vision that could catapult his company, Vidyah, into becoming the fastest-growing software company of all-time. Bill is an Impact Leader, and here's how he is executing on his vision.

There is a seismic shift going on in distance learning, or e-learning. Bill Mundell has been a leader in this field, with his digital delivery system for distance learning and his innovative "outside in" marketing approach.

In the United States, e-learning has been seen as a cost-cutting method for corporate training. In China, it is a societal necessity. Vidyah recently signed a contract with the government of China ensuring that the Vidyah delivery system will be deployed in over 630,000 schools throughout China over the next five years!

I think when the largest non-democratic country in the world's social stability depends on delivering education, that incentive is every bit as powerful an incentive as the profit motive is to explore new technologies that can solve their problem.

—William Mundell, chairman and CEO, Vidyah

Students hungry for education have overwhelmed China's traditional education system, its teachers and schools. Students are looking for affordable access to distance learning. Herein lies the opportunity for Vidyah to establish itself as the e-learning software standard in China.

The Chinese government has been working on how to use technology to supply affordable content to its people for many years. China has developed an elaborate fiber-and-satellite network, giving their educational institutions the most sophisticated broadband network in the world. The missing piece was a delivery platform. Bill Mundell saw this opportunity and decided that a market driven by "social needs" would be more receptive to innovation than a market driven by cost savings—hence his success in marketing his product to China.

Now with a stronghold in China, he is pursuing other opportunities in Asia, a geographic region that is more advanced than the United States or Western Europe in its use of broadband. For example, South Korea has the eleventh largest economy in the world, but it has the largest number of broadband users.

With its innovative delivery platform and innovative marketing approach, which focused on Asia first, now Vidyah is ready to become the delivery standard in the United States and Western Europe.

William Mundell's Biography

William Mundell, chairman and chief executive officer of Vidyah, founded the company with partners from Knowledge Universe, Michael Milken and Larry Ellison, to create the next generation e-learning model.

He previously served as president and CEO of WEFA Group, where he executed a series of strategic acquisitions that consolidated the economic information industry and turned WEFA into an international organization. In 1997, with assistance from Bain Capital, he was able to engineer the sale of WEFA and create exceptional returns to WEFA shareholders.

He also served as chairman of Trade, Inc., a leading company in international trade information, financed by Sutter Hill and Bain Capital. He was an adjunct professor at UCLA's Anderson Graduate School of Management, where he taught economics and finance. He has authored articles in The Wall Street Journal, The New York Times *and* The Financial Times, *and he is a contributing editor to* International Trade *and* International Banking.

Bill has a BS in Economics and Political Science from Carlton University and MBA and MIA degrees from Columbia University.

Dot #3: Embrace Innovation and Change to Better Serve All Stakeholders

Innovation Is the Only Way to Create New Wealth and Shape Society. Continuous Performance Improvement Depends on Novelty.

Federal Reserve Chairman Alan Greenspan spoke to the Society of Business Economists in London on September 25, 2002:

> A never-ending stream of innovation has led inexorably to expanded trade and improved productivity in many nations throughout the world. Today, we can see on the horizon vast new means of communicating and computing, practical applications of advances of biotechnology, and doubtless many other innovations. But a half-century from now, the goods and services that we produce and consume will, to a significant extent, reflect applications of insights not yet formed or even imagined.

Innovation is everything. When you're on the forefront, you can see what the next innovation needs to be.

—Robert Noyce, founder, Intel

Brand Innovation

Many people today equate innovation only with technology or bioscience. The truth is that traditional companies with high-brand equity products have an enormous opportunity to create wealth for themselves through innovation. Traditional companies must embrace innovation in their organization to do so.

Innovate by saying something new about something old, says Brendan Foley of the H. J. Heinz Company.

Brendan Foley

H. J. Heinz: An Innovative and High-Impact Player

He who rejects change is the architect of decay.
—Harold Wilson, former British prime minister

Brendan Foley, general manager for condiments of the H. J. Heinz Company, tells a simple but fascinating story about the innovation of new types of ketchup and its packaging at the Innovators 2002 Conference.

"Heinz Ketchup is about fun. It's about being thick and rich. It's about our icon glass bottle. That bottle signifies what Heinz Ketchup is to many people, because they see it every day on tabletops in restaurants, even though we don't sell this bottle in retail grocery and we haven't for years. But that association is pretty strong. And many people associate Heinz with the song "Anticipation." Some people even think that we're still running that advertising because it registered that well.

"Now, from a kid's perspective, Heinz ketchup is still thick and rich. They love the texture of the product. It's still fun. But they live in a world of color. They watch Nickelodeon, watch the WB Network. For them, it's all about color. And they like to play with their food. Adults may not do that anymore, but kids do. With kids, heritage is probably, maximum, two years, right? When it comes to "Anticipation," they've probably never heard the song. And they may not even notice that our glass bottle exists. So from a kid's perspective, this brand really had a lot of open territory.

"From kids' perspective—and we asked a lot of them—there are no boundaries. The only thing we had to deliver was the same taste, because they love the taste of Heinz Ketchup. Don't screw with that, they told us. But everything else was fair game. So we came up with Heinz EZ Squirt. And I think, by now, everyone has seen it or probably has a bottle in their refrigerator.

"Ironically, the real genesis behind this idea was not to make ketchup green or purple or pink. Color was a promotional play. The real power behind this idea was when kids in focus groups came back to us and said, 'I want the ketchup that draws.' That was the real leading idea here.

"This product was designed by kids and for kids. They told us they wanted a streamlined bottle, something they could hold in their hands. Now, we didn't want the bottle to be too small, because that means Mom would have to run back and forth between the grocery store way too often, but a streamlined bottle so they could hold it very easily and a nozzle that squirted out ketchup in a thin stream.

"Now, that's a little bit counterintuitive. You'd think consumption would go down if you made the stream smaller because you couldn't squirt as much out.

Actually, it has the opposite effect. It's such a cool thing to witness a kid watching the stream come out of the bottle. They just keep squirting and squirting and squirting.

"Next we asked the kids, 'What could we do to really dial this thing up?' And they said, 'Make it a different color.' We didn't come up with that idea. Kids gave us that idea. They asked for it. We initially thought, there's no way. How do you go before senior management and the board of directors and suggest that?

"So we really researched the heck out of the idea. The whole idea of color is really that kids draw, kids paint, and that's kind of where it brought it home for them and really delivered the whole idea of control and expression. And they knew their moms and dads would not like to eat green ketchup. It would be made just for them.

"Of course, we wanted to reassure moms, and they were very positive about it in focus groups. Ketchup is a product that's used on everything. It's all about tomatoes. But when you make something green, you've got to make sure it's okay with parents. Also, fortification is important these days in a lot of our product categories. So we fortified it with Vitamin C.

"The type of publicity that we got on the EZ Squirt launch was amazing. Our PR experts tell us it was second only to Viagra in buzz when it came out. It was a media storm of. It was worth millions in advertising dollars.

"It's important in this kind of environment to really connect yourself with the things that are hot with your consumers. With kids, it's Cartoon Network, getting on the Internet with those properties, Nickelodeon, the WB Network.

"One really fun thing we did was a campaign that came out of Burger King. They called us and said they wanted to go with this green ketchup. Now they're one of our top food service customers. We were really energized that they were excited about the idea. They called their whole campaign 'Choose the ooze,' and everything they sold was green. It was one of their best promotions they have had. A lot of the franchises were writing in, saying, 'This is driving a lot of traffic.' So connecting it back to the food service environment was successful.

"Another successful marketing opportunity came our way when we got a call saying Steven Spielberg wanted some green ketchup for a party he was having to promote his movie *Shrek* in the L.A. area. We figured this was a match made in heaven. When *Shrek* was coming out, we had just launched green ketchup. So we put Shrek and Princess Fiona on our bottles. And then that kind of led all the way to the *Grinch*. We did a Christmas promotion with Warner Bros. in that movie. It resulted in a lot of great tie-ins with a lot of great characters and properties.

"Then, in 2002, we came out with Mystery Color. The whole idea there was that you didn't know what color was inside the bottle until you opened it. Tremendously successful. We ran three colors: Awesome Orange, Passion Pink, and Totally Teal. And so it really kind of helped elevate the idea of the surprise factor and the real personalization that you could have with this product.

"We also took EZ Squirt global; we have launched the product in Australia, the U.K., Canada, the Netherlands, Germany, and also in some of the markets in South America. Again, in many cases, the products really drove a lot of excitement and created a halo effect on their categories, as well as being ketchup leaders in their respective countries. So it was really a globally simple idea.

"Here's the thing you have to keep in mind: The size of the child's hands, whether they're in Sweden or they're in the U.S., is basically the same. The need for control and independence is basically the same. A lot of the insights and the principles were re-applied very quickly. When you think about it, you're breaking down the barriers of culture. They all love ketchup. They're all kids. They're all going to act generally the same way with the product.

"Now, about results. At H. J. Heinz Company, we are very focused on results. We captured five additional share points in about a year after the EZ Squirt green launch. In a $600 million category, capturing five percent, completely incremental, is great stuff. That really helped drive the category.

"Now, this isn't just about EZ Squirt sales. What happened was there was a huge halo effect on the base business. New products, new innovations, even if it's an extension, really do provide a halo effect on the overall brand and the overall sales.

"It creates excitement and interest in the category again. And if you didn't go to the store and buy green ketchup, you were probably thinking about ketchup a little bit more frequently than you were before, and that's the news value.

"EZ Squirt drove half of our share growth that first year. The rest of it came from our base business. It wasn't cannibalistic at all, which is very exciting.

"And when you think about share, which is something we track weekly, we started off being below versus a year ago, by about two points overall. But as we laid out new pricing and the new advertising campaign—meaning fixing the basics—share started to go up. Then you look at the "trap cap" innovation. Again, we started driving share growth even further. And then we came in with even further innovation behind EZ Squirt purple. You can see the effects on the share of the business. Continued sustained growth.

"And I think it kind of ends with, well, how did we end up versus our goal? We wanted to be at fifty percent share or higher to the sum of the volume basis. Well, we ended up fiscal year 2002 at fifty-four percent, the highest volume share ever in the history of our business. We have since hit a sixty share in terms of dollars—also a company record.

"So we achieved great results through a lot of hard work. You might think it comes easy, but this is over three years, and it doesn't stop there, because you have to keep churning that growth. But that's what it's going to take: continuous innovation.

"So how do we continue to do that? Well, we came out with the Ketchup Kick'rs—flavored ketchup—in February 2002. What's happening here is that adults are not eating as much ketchup. It might be a combination of how many hamburgers they're eating these days as opposed to when they were children, but it's also about the taste profile, too. Adults like bolder flavors.

"So we came out with Ketchup Kick'rs. We haven't even passed our six-month mark, but we're doing quite well. We've captured at least 2 or 2.5 or 3 percent dollar share of the market just so far.

"So—a great innovation, really going after a new segment of the marketplace, which is young adults and those who have kind of fallen off in ketchup consumption. "And then there is the upside-down bottle—Heinz Easy Squeeze. This is really borne out of a consumer insight as well, and that is, how many times have you taken your bottle of ketchup and turned it upside down in your refrigerator to get it all out? Kind of annoying, isn't it? Well, how do you solve that? Turn it upside down. In fact, every squeeze is like your first squeeze when you take that bottle out, no matter how many times you've used it.

"What we have is a patented silicone valve cap, which controls the squirt, because when you have it hanging upside down, you don't want the ketchup coming out of the bottle. When you try it at home, it is a superior performing package, and it really takes care of the dissatisfaction that some consumers had with our package. When you think about things that annoy or bother consumers, those become real opportunities for you if you solve them!

"The lessons: **Be an entrepreneur.** I think there was a saying back a couple years ago when the dot-com businesses were really hot: You're in the old economy business, not the new economy. That made me realize that we've got to start thinking about our brands in a refreshing 'new economy' manner every single day. We have to innovate, innovate, innovate all the time. You have to think about it as an entrepreneur. When someone says you can't do it, then that should give you the license to go ahead and see that you really can.

"**Change before you have to.** If you don't take the lead, someone else will. Take some risks. You have to innovate. Fix the fundamentals first. Don't take your eye off the fundamentals that drive consumers: pricing, product preference, and product superiority. You have to take care of those first before you really target innovation.

"**And then, lastly—and this is probably the most important point—know your real consumer, that end user.** This, frankly, would not all have come about if we didn't really pay attention to what kids were saying, really observe them, really spend a lot of time watching how they act, watching how they behave with the product, and listening to what they're looking for and looking at it from their perspective."

The Impact Player Challenge™

The credit belongs to the man who is actually in the arena...who strives valiantly, who knows the great enthusiasms, the great devotions, and spends himself in worthy causes. Who, at best, knows the triumph of high achievement and who, at worst, if he fails, fails while daring greatly so that his place shall never be with those cold and timid souls who know neither victory or defeat.

—President Theodore Roosevelt

THE IMMEDIATE GOAL

To help 10,000 people maximize their success the first year and 100,000 every year thereafter.

THE LONG-TERM GOAL

To develop an international network of Impact Players who are interested in maximizing their success and the success of others.

Success in business requires training and discipline and hard work. But if you're not frightened by these things, the opportunities are just as great today as they ever were.

—David Rockefeller, philanthropist

The **Impact Player Institute™** believes that most business people strive for Continuous Performance Improvement. We also believe that many people don't understand what it takes for CPI. That's why we developed The Impact Player Challenge. The Impact Player Challenge is a step-by-step program enabling people to become the best that they can be.

The Ten-Step Impact Player Challenge

Becoming an Impact Player requires an "inside-out" approach. You have to understand your strengths and play to them. You also have to be motivated and passionate. That's the only way true transformation occurs. It requires effort. First, you must commit to understanding your strengths. I mean really commit to it—act like your life depends on it, because it does. Are you ready to take The Impact Player Challenge? Good—let's move forward.

Step 1—The Commitment

Step 1 is to start a journal now. A notebook will work. This journal will stay with you for your entire journey. It will become part of your life, because the quality of your life depends on it. On the cover, write your name in bold under the words "Impact Player" and "Continuous Performance Improvement." Below are the questions that only you can answer and that only you will see. Be honest and write the answers to these questions after you have written down today's date. Yes, now is the time to become an Impact Player.

1) Are you ready for Continuous Performance Improvement and to become an Impact Player right now?

2) Are you ready to play to your strengths and develop them every day?

3) Are you ready to embrace innovation and change?

4) Are you ready to develop a network of leaders from diverse backgrounds?

5) Are you ready to build your life around your strengths?

6) Are you really ready to change the way you think, the way you see the world, the way you view others?

7) Are you ready to sacrifice your current comfort zone and embrace new ideas?

8) Are you ready to push yourself to grow?

9) Are you ready to treat change as an opportunity?

10) Are you ready to create value and help others?

11) Are you ready to surround yourself with Impact Players?

12) Are you ready to set deadlines and reach goals?

13) Are you ready to finish what you start?

14) Are you ready to lead by example?

15) Are you ready to reach your potential?

16) Are you ready to transform yourself from the inside out?

17) Are you ready for a life-changing experience?

18) Are you ready to ask for help when needed?

19) Are you ready to strive for a more satisfying life?

20) Are you ready to overcome the challenges that life will throw your way?

If you answered yes to all those questions, you're ready to become an Impact Player. If you answered no to one or more, I suggest rereading this book, then retaking this questionnaire.

Step 2—Impact Player Defined

Write the attributes of an Impact Player (below) in your journal and on two index cards. One of the cards is for home and the other is for work. Please read them in the morning, at lunch, and at night.

I am an Impact Player because I have the:

> ➢ Talent necessary for the job I have chosen.
>
> ➢ Motivation to excel at my work.
>
> ➢ Energy to execute my plan.
>
> ➢ Vision to know where I'm going.
>
> ➢ Self-discipline to work long hours and be persistent.
>
> ➢ Burning passion for excellence.
>
> ➢ Emotional intensity that positively impacts others.
>
> ➢ Commitment to serve others.
>
> ➢ Vision to see change as an opportunity.
>
> ➢ Goal to be a person of character, faith, and courage.
>
> ➢ Understanding of the importance of diversity.
>
> ➢ Correct self-assessment of my skills and motivations, which allows me to set goals that are specific, attainable, measurable, reviewable, and trackable.

From time to time it will be important to come back to *Connect the Dots... To Become an Impact Player* and review the major tenets of the book.

Step 3—Discover Your Impact Niche

Now it's time to understand your strengths and motivations in order to focus on your Impact Niche. There are two ways to go about doing this.

1) You can write in your journal what you think your strengths and motivators are, or

2) You can use a professional instrument called the Impact Player Assessment. The engine of this assessment tool was originally funded by a grant from the Justice Department. This instrument will measure you strengths (a combination of talents and motivations) against a database of more than 400,000 individuals. It can be found at **www.ImpactPlayer.net**.

Step 4—Write Down Your Goals

List your top ten goals and how you are going to achieve them.

Step 5—Plan for Tomorrow

Every evening before you go to bed, write down what you did that day that helped move you toward being an Impact Player. Also, write down one thing you are going to do the next day that will help you develop your Impact Niche.

Step 6—Transformation by Emulation

Pick out an Impact Player (living or crossed over) you respect and want to emulate. Read about that person's life and emulate it.

Step 7—Develop Your Business Network

Expand your Impact Player Network. Join an organization or association that will place you among other Impact Players. Make sure this organization's membership consists of a diverse group of Impact Players. Don't let geographic barriers stop you from joining a group. The organization we started is The Impact Player League. More information can be found at **www.ImpactPlayer.net**.

Step 8—Envision Success

Spend five minutes during the day with your eyes closed envisioning how well you are progressing. Focus on the positive steps you have made, not how far you have to go.

Step 9—Congratulate yourself

Every day, congratulate yourself first thing in the morning and right before you go to bed on being a winner. Review the transformation you are going through. Focus on the progress you have made, not how far you have to go.

Step 10—The Impact Player Coin (optional)

Purchase an Impact Player Challenge Coin to carry around with you. The Impact Player Challenge coin is a physical representation of the commitment to change into an Impact Player. When you awake and go about your daily tasks, the coin is a reminder to do your very best and become an Impact Player by preparing yourself for change and challenge. At the start of the day, place the coin in your left pocket. When you complete a task that brings you closer to becoming an Impact Player, move the coin to the right pocket. At the end of every day, the coin should come out of the right pocket. Impact Player Challenge Coins be purchased at **www.ImpactPlayer.net**.

Our Assessment Partner: The HR Chally Group

Knowing your strengths and motivations is a major part of Continuous Performance Improvement and the Impact Challenges. Choosing the proper assessment instrument and company was a major decision for The Impact Player Institute. Once we met the professionals from The HR Chally Group, we knew we had found the right partner.

"Success Can Be Predicted"

One of the leading companies in the field of predictive assessments is The HR Chally Group, based in Dayton, Ohio. The HR Chally Group was founded in 1973 through a grant from the U.S. Justice Department to develop non-discriminatory and predictive selection assessment methods.

Chally competencies include collecting qualitative information as well as quantitative data from job candidates, employees, and customers to provide quantifiable statistics that can be analyzed and converted to predictive information. These can then be used to make accurate and objective business decisions. Chally's methods have been thoroughly tested and applied to more than 400,000 sales-and-management candidates. Today, Chally serves over 2,000 clients globally in all business segments. Chally clients include General Motors, Corporate Express, Reynolds & Reynolds, Emmis Communications, and The South Financial Group.

* Note: For example of The Impact Player Assessment, please go to the APPENDIX section in the back of this book.

Part 2

Inspiration

Impact Players and Their Inspirational Interviews

Here is your chance to meet regular people, just like you and me, who are doing extraordinary things. We hope their missions influence you to take chances and aim your sights a little higher, and inspire you to become an Impact Player and surround yourself with other Impact Players.

Diane Swonk

Diane Swonk: "The Passionate Economist" on Adapting to Change

The *Merriam-Webster Dictionary* defines the word "context" as "the interrelated conditions in which something exists or occurs." According to Impact Player Diane Swonk, context is a word all of us should become intimately aware of in our attempt to lead successful lives.

Contextually, all of us live in a state of constant change. Continuous movement defines our lives. We are the same person, but we must continually learn and adapt. If we stop learning and adapting, we face extinction.

Diane says, "Our surroundings (the context in which we live) define the ease at which we conduct our daily lives. As human beings, we look for normalcy in our lives. We try to extrapolate the future by looking at the immediate past. We don't like when the rules of the game change." Unfortunately for those who don't like change, the context of our lives is in a state of constant rearrangement.

On September 11, 2001, Diane learned just how quickly and brutally the rules of the game can change. Diane was at the annual meeting of the National Association for Business Economics (NABE) at the World Trade Center that day. In fact, she had selected the site herself in 1998, during her rise to the presidency of NABE.

On September 11th, the context of the entire world changed dramatically, and Diane Swonk was a firsthand witness. She remembers the morning weather of September 11th in New York as beautiful. Unfortunately, her day was hectic and she was too busy to enjoy the moment. She was late for breakfast and had already done a TV interview.

Between the time she heard the tinkling of chandeliers, which began to shake from the force of a plane hitting the building, and her return to Chicago fifty-two hours later, her life changed forever. Luckier than many, Diane was on the ground floor and got out quickly, but she had a surreal day, covered in dust, searching for friends to make sure they were all right, and most of all, needing to be with her family so they could reassure one another.

Diane's harrowing ordeal is with her every day as she relives the mental images of people jumping in pairs, holding hands to comfort each other as they tried to escape the inferno. If any good can come out of that experience, it's that Diane's clear values were completely and unequivocally reinforced. She is in awe of the power of the human spirit. She says the resilience of the American people and our economy are truly special.

Diane has some ideas on dealing with change and challenge:

1) Focus on the present.
2) Keep sight of your passions.

3) Be true to yourself.

4) Understand that life is multidimensional and our experiences are interrelated.

5) Embrace change.

Diane suggests that all of us have something to learn about our interrelationships around the globe: "If one theme should resonate from September 11th, it is that the lives of our children are desperately dependent upon how children around the world view their own fates."

As for Diane, she and her family are doing fine. Diane never told her children her experience of September 11. They read about it in her book, *The Passionate Economist*. While doing a school project, Diane's daughter Madison was asked by her teacher months after September 11 what made her unique. Her reply: "I don't ever give up."

Diane Swonk's Biography

Diane Swonk is director of economics, chief economist, and senior vice president at Bank One Corporation in Chicago, where she manages the bank's Corporate Economics Group. She is a clinical professor in DePaul University's MBA program. She recently published her first book, The Passionate Economist: Finding the Power and Humanity behind the Numbers.

Swonk began her career with First Chicago Corporation. She is a national economics consultant and appears regularly on TV and in major financial publications. She serves on the board of the National Association for Business Economics (NABE and the Finance Committee of the Executive Club of Chicago), and is a director of the Illinois Economic Education Association. She was named "Business Leader of the Year" by the YWCA of Metropolitan Chicago and NABE Fellow for her contributions to business economics. Swonk was one of The Wall Street Journal's *"Star Forecasters" and was named "Top Woman in Finance in Chicago" by* Today's Chicago Woman. *She earned her master's in Economics with honors from the University of Michigan and her MBA with honors from the University of Chicago.*

Dick Traum

Dick Traum: Successful People Overcome Serious Situations by Being Passionate and Focused on Achievement

When you are disabled, you learn very quickly that we are all brothers and sisters on this planet. Race, religion, gender, political orientation and ethnicity all evaporate in the shared experiences of the disabled.

—Dick Traum

Dick Traum established the Achilles Track Club (ATC) in 1983 to encourage disabled people to participate in long-distance running with the general public. Dick is its president and the first leg amputee in the world to complete a marathon.

For Dick, losing part of his leg was a speed bump on the road to a successful life. "I was twenty-four years old, finishing my Ph.D., and had things to accomplish in life. My leg was not a tremendous part of my life. Losing part of my leg was not a big issue. It happened, I had a little down time, and then it was time to move forward and go on in life."

Success, Dick says, is having control over one's life. "You have to position yourself where you have control. For example, I have always paid for my own education, college and advanced degrees. At eighteen years of age, I started a soda business where I had three trucks. Then, in 1970, I built a consulting company. I had no one to report to. My successes and failures would point back to me. The degree of success was always in direct correlation to the effort I put into it."

"Since its founding in New York City, the Achilles Track Club has expanded into forty chapters in the United States and more than 110 chapters on six continents, including countries such as Norway, New Zealand, Mongolia, the Dominican Republic, Russia, South Africa, Vietnam, and Japan.

"Achilles includes people with all kinds of disabilities, such as visual impairment, the residual effects of stroke, cerebral palsy, paraplegia, arthritis, amputation, multiple sclerosis, cystic fibrosis, cancer, traumatic head injury, and many others. Runners participate with crutches, in wheelchairs, on prostheses, or without aids.

"Achilles provides biweekly training programs at most chapters. In New York City, in association with the Office of Adaptive Physical Education of the NYC Board of Education and the Department of Parks and Recreation, the group trains 2,000 disadvantaged children with disabilities at fifty public schools. This year, a new program for disabled seniors at senior citizen centers, Achilles 65, has begun. Programs in conjunction with other organizations provide eye surgery for blind runners, below-the-knee prostheses, and sports wheelchairs for Achilles members.

"Achilles is involved in many local and national running events. Every year, the group sponsors a large number of disabled runners from around the world for the New York City Marathon."

Members of ATC have overcome serious obstacles. Dick feels it is far more important for people to listen than to give advice to people coping with the toughest problems. Support groups, prayer, and feedback help people gain control of their lives again after serious situations arise. Mary Bryant, a Ford model and volunteer at ATC, was back on the fashion runway just weeks after a mastectomy. Group support was the key.

Some serious situations require years of support and prayers. Trisha Meili is the chairperson for ATC. She is also known as The Central Park Jogger, the woman who was brutally beaten, raped, and left for dead in 1989. According to Dick Traum, Trisha credits prayer from thousands of strangers as well as friends for her ability to come back. Her 2003 book, *I Am the Central Park Jogger*, is a must-read for anyone interested in the power of the human spirit.

Dick believes that people who are passionate and achievement-oriented lead successful lives. When you put people like that in a team environment, their performance is maximized. People who are passionate enjoy interacting with others. Passionate people have an affinity for serving others. He sees the benefits of group membership all the time at the Achilles Track Club. People always run faster when part of a team.

Dick believes that the true leaders in our society are natural group members. They enjoy serving others on their team. There is no doubt in his mind that community, cohesiveness, and success go hand in hand. Leaders are passionate and focused on the achievement of the team. Success and service to others cannot be separated.

Governor Martha Layne Collins

Governor Martha Layne Collins: Always on Duty, Always on Call

Service to others is the rent you pay for your room here on Earth.
—Muhammad Ali

Growing up in the funeral-home and ambulance-service businesses prepared Martha Layne Collins for life. She learned that life is uncertain, and you must be always on duty and always on call. There were no major highways where she grew up, just a two-lane road that always seemed to produce an emergency as the family was leaving on vacation. From her parents she learned that helping people came before vacations or a good night's sleep. She also learned that all people should be helped and treated the same, no matter which side of the tracks they are from. Raised in this manner, it was natural that Martha Layne Collins would become a leader by serving others.

As governor of Kentucky from 1983 to 1987, she was noted for education reform and visionary economic-development policies. "The simultaneous emphasis on education and economic development is a natural," Governor Collins says. "They are interrelated. If you have a trained and educated workforce, companies will come, the tax base will increase, and educational institutions and communities will benefit."

She believes in developing relationships with a diverse group of people and having all the members of a team understand how their roles fit into the overall organizational focus. Even as a child, she learned the value of global reach from the Christian missionaries.

Governor Collins' leadership style proved a boon to Kentucky's economy. An economic study recommended that Kentucky target the auto industry because of the state's location and workforce. She immediately visited automakers in Japan to establish a relationship. She was adamant that something new be built in Kentucky; she did not want to steal anything from another region.

In Japan, she called on Toyota. (She was the only woman in the room.) The company had not said anything about building anything new in North America, yet she knew that it was worth her time and energy to build a relationship, just in case. Her vision and strategy paid off. Once Toyota announced its plans to build a plant in North America, every economic development official in the United States went to Japan to court Toyota, but Governor Collins had already established a relationship with them. The plant went to Georgetown, Kentucky.

Governor Martha Layne Collins prides herself on being a mentor. She wants people to discover how to be successful. She is bothered by people who are unhappy in this world because they are in the wrong position, the proverbial square pegs in the round holes. One of her first questions when mentoring someone is, "Tell me what you like and don't like. You have to like what you do to be successful." She is as tough on young people as she is on herself and instills in them the desire to be the best they can be.

When someone works with Governor Collins, she gives him or her lots of information. Then she helps them discover how what they're doing is important to the overall objective of the team. Team members understand the big picture. Next, she empowers them to do their jobs. This empowerment pushes their limits. Governor Collins believes that people have to be comfortable with what they're doing, even with some level of anxiety. Trial and error is the ultimate teacher. Positive experiences then build self-esteem, which in turn helps people reach their potential. Asking questions is a sign of confidence—something she emphasizes especially to women, who too often think admitting what they don't know, is a sign of weakness.

Finally, she encourages everyone to build relationships with people. If that means travel, then by all means, go on the road. In any organization, people need to be part of a team. People need assignments, a time frame, and an awareness of the expectations people have of them. People work better when they understand the big picture.

Currently, Governor Martha Layne Collins is providing her leadership to Georgetown College as executive scholar in residence. Her focus is on students learning the interrelationships of business, political science, culture, and a global economy. To help meet that objective, all students are required to study a foreign language. She knows that when people are exposed to other cultures, they become better at what they do. Economic development depends on education, innovation, and relationships.

To remain an innovative institution of higher education Georgetown College has developed the Commerce, Language, and Culture Studies program (CLC). Here's how the program is described: "Georgetown College recognizes that business and culture are inextricably linked. Opportunities for students to participate in the global society and to engage effectively in business will be enhanced if students have studied business, language, and culture in an integrated and reflective manner." In the course description, it's obvious that business, language, and culture classes form the foundation of future successful business executives. Governor Collins knows that the true business leaders of tomorrow will understand who people are as well as what numbers mean.

What's next for Governor Martha Layne Collins? Who knows? But one thing is certain. Whoever she works with will receive the best possible leadership. Because just like the young girl that helped accident victims and families in times of need, Governor Martha Layne Collins is always on duty and always on call to serve others.

Martha Layne Collins' Biography

Martha Layne Collins grew up in Shelby County, Kentucky, graduated from The University of Kentucky, and worked as a schoolteacher until 1970. She then worked as coordinator of women's activities in several Democratic political campaigns, which led her to run for office. In 1978 and 1979, she served as clerk of the Supreme Court of the Commonwealth of Kentucky, where she guided the office through the most far-reaching changes in the history of the state's judicial system.

Lieutenant governor from 1979 to 1983, she sat as president of the State Senate and as vice chair and chair of the National Conference of Lieutenant Governors. She gained critical experience in leadership while actively serving as governor. She was elected the first woman governor of the Commonwealth in 1983.

Barred by law from running for re-election, she went on to serve as president of St. Catharine College for six years, as executive in residence at the University of Louisville's School of Business, and as director of the International Business and Management Center at the University of Kentucky's Carol Martin Gatton College of Business and Economics. Governor Collins was a Harvard University Fellow in the John F. Kennedy School of Government at the Institute of Politics in Cambridge, Massachusetts.

Since 1998, Governor Collins has served as executive scholar in residence at Georgetown College, Georgetown, Kentucky. She is on the boards of directors of Eastman Kodak Company and R. R. Donnelly and Sons, and she is an advisory board member of BB&T and Anthem Blue Cross/Blue Shield. She is married to Dr. Bill L. Collins and enjoys the company of her children and grandchildren.

Neil Bush

Neil Bush: Giving Children a Chance to Learn the Way They Learn Best

We have the greatest institutions of higher learning in the world. Our universities are magnets for students from around the world. The real problem is K-12. Kids get out of high school and they can't even read.
— **Richard Cavanagh, president and CEO,**
The Conference Board

Please meet Neil Bush. Yes, the same Neil Bush whose father, George Herbert Walker Bush, was the forty-first president of the United States; whose mother, Barbara Bush, is mother and grandmother to an entire country; whose brother George W. Bush is the forty-third president of the United States and leader of the free world. The Bushes are a family of Impact Players. Overcoming adversity is a major characteristic of Impact Players. Neil Bush overcame dyslexia. He is now on a leadership-and-innovation mission to fix our broken education system. Success to Neil is having a positive impact on children's lives.

Middle-school reality

The school system is failing miserably, especially middle-school education. Our educational approach in the United States hasn't changed in 200 years, even though we live in a completely different world. Textbooks, conformity, and eight-hour school days are the norm. If our kids don't conform, we drug them with Ritalin.

Pierce Bush, Neil's son, was misdiagnosed with Attention Deficit Disorder (ADD). Pierce refused to be drugged, so a professional learning assessment was done. The outcome: "Gifted."

Neil and Pierce are full-fledged Impact Players. Neil is developing a new education delivery system to help kids learn the way they learn best. He calls his company Ignite! Learning.

Neil and I met with John Pepper when he was chairman of Procter & Gamble, the undisputed leader in consumer products and market research. Neil discussed his approach to education. John agreed with Neil that children are "the consumers of education" and that the best way to build a successful product is to give the consumers what they want. Neil Bush is giving children a choice on how they want to learn. Let's read Neil's story in his own words.

Neil Bush's Story

My life is my message.

—**Gandhi**

"Ignite! was founded in 1999 on the core beliefs that all kids can learn—they just learn differently—that learning is best accomplished by doing, and that technology is a potentially powerful tool that, if properly harnessed, can lead to teacher success and light up learning for middle-school students.

"The motivation for founding Ignite! grew out of very personal experiences, specifically, the experience of being a dyslexic student myself and struggling in grade school, and later observing the experiences our three children had in middle school.

"I was raised in Houston, Texas, and had a charming personality that served me well in elementary school. Hugs, smiles, and a disposition to work hard helped me to get passing grades in all subjects. In third grade, when the skill of reading became more important for success in school, my grades began to slide.

"My mother tells of a time when I was recovering from an illness at home and she asked me to read from a simple book to her. I struggled and literally could not read through the book. Mom reported this observation to the educators at the public school I was attending, and she was reassured that I could in fact read. They invited her to attend a class to observe for herself.

"We were sitting in a circle on the floor, taking turns reading. My turn came. The words did not flow. Silence was replaced by my neighbor's whispering the words for me to repeat, then the coaching of the teacher, both of them filling in what I couldn't do for myself. My mother and I both knew the truth.

"In part because of this reading disability and in part because of the way instruction was delivered, I have scarred memories of sitting in boring classrooms, disconnected from the lectures, suffering anxiety over tests, hating having to rely on textbooks.

"What really galvanized my interest in starting Ignite! was seeing our three children's school experiences. Our daughters are wonderfully studious, pleaser-type students who cruised through elementary school and patiently, steadily labored through middle school, without joy in the academics but without complaint.

"Our son, who is more the hunter-warrior type, is sandwiched between the two girls. He has a powerful personality and a real gift for connecting with others. Pierce has been on *Larry King Live* twice and has been interviewed on other national television shows.

"When you speak with him about a subject he cares about or watch him on TV, you would conclude that Pierce has a gift, a powerful intelligence, and that he must be an straight-A student. Pierce charmed his way through elementary school, but in middle school he started doing more and more poorly. The principal of the school and a couple of independent counselors diagnosed Pierce with ADD and prescribed that he take Ritalin to help with his focus.

"Pierce refused to take Ritalin. This forced us to seek an alternative diagnosis. Pierce underwent a thorough evaluation at the Howard School in Atlanta, where we were informed not of his disabilities but of his gifts.

"The evaluators suggested that I read books by developmental psychologist Howard Gardner on the theory of multiple intelligences, books about constructivist theory, and books about the abundant brain research on learning.

"Over the next six months, I read books and established strongly-held core beliefs that would drive the development activities at Ignite! The first of these beliefs is that all kids can learn, they just learn differently. The second is that learning is best accomplished by doing things and applying concepts, a shift from the "memorize and forget" model. And finally, we believe that technology can be a powerful tool when properly harnessed in engaging kids to learn the way they learn best.

"With the mission of developing a practical solution to help middle-school teachers succeed in public schools, Ignite! is publishing comprehensive courseware and content that aligns with state and national standards and that is designed around how research shows kids learn best.

"It takes some courage to try to penetrate a market dominated by an oligopoly of textbook publishers. But because our solution goes way beyond textbooks, engaging kids through the use of videos, songs, rhythms, rhymes, pictures, text, and manipulative entities, and because we build in project-oriented learning experiences, we are providing teachers with a transformationally better way to connect with kids.

"Will we succeed in crossing the chasm into the mainstream of our marketplace? The answer is yes. Why? Because of leadership. Leadership is about listening to the marketplace and reacting in a practical way to meet the integral needs of that market. Leadership is about knowing that what you are doing is going to make a huge difference in the lives of your customer and working like mad to prove that your vision is rooted in reality. Leadership is about persevering in the face of high barriers such as terrible capital markets and a complacent, bureaucratic marketplace.

"We have seen why others with technology solutions in education have failed. We have seen why others with curricular approaches have failed. And we use this critical information to show us how we will succeed!

"In three to five years, Ignite! will quietly establish our presence in the public school market as a leader in providing truly engaging and effective comprehensive courseware."

Neil Bush's Biography

Neil Bush is chairman and CEO of Ignite! Inc., a company he founded in March of 1999. Ignite! has designed an online curriculum publishing and delivery system for middle school teachers and administrators who are feeling the pressure to improve student performance and use installed technology in schools. Ignite!'s engaging, standards-based curriculum will help teachers teach and will capitalize on each child's learning potential to improve student performance.

Neil has over twenty years of diversified executive experience in energy, investment banking, technology, and political campaigns. At Ignite!, the mission of improving learning performance by recognizing and addressing each individual's unique strengths arises out of Neil's sincere commitment to a thoughtful, positive reformation of our nation's K-12 education system.

Neil received a BS in International Economics from Tulane University and an MBA from the Tulane University School of Business. He serves on the boards of The Points of Light Foundation and of the George Bush School of Public Service, a graduate program on the campus of Texas A&M.

Fred Scrutchfield with country music superstar Toby Keith

Fred Scrutchfield: A Waring Blender with a Successful Recipe for Mixing Business with Pleasure

The human race has only one effective weapon—and that is laughter.
—Mark Twain

When you attend a Fred Scrutchfield event you'll be amazed at the mix of Impact Players from business, entertainment, government, non-profit organizations, and professional sports. Fred's events are magnificent productions that combine golf, live music, and quite a bit of business conversation. Fred's motto is, "After a round of golf and sharing good music, your customers will treat you like a member of the family." The result is a relationship-building experience second to none.

You shouldn't be surprised—after all, Fred Scrutchfield learned his trade from world-class entertainer Fred Waring. Mr. Waring was a showman and entrepreneur extraordinaire for over fifty years. He and his band, Fred Waring and the Pennsylvanians, could be heard and seen on radio, records, and television. Smart sponsors lined up for his programs and Mr. Waring even developed his own line of appliances. The Waring Blender led the way.

The year was 1963 and the place was Shawnee-on-Delaware, Pennsylvania: a golf resort eighty-five miles from New York City located in the Pocono's and owned by Fred Waring. The new director of public relations was Fred Scrutchfield. Celebrities including Frank Sinatra and Bing Crosby vacationed there. Jackie Gleason was so fond of the resort that he lived there in the summer. Fred Scrutchfield played golf with and learned from all of them. One of Fred's favorites was Dinah Shore. He and Dinah met there and built a friendship that would last a lifetime.

In 1980, Fred Scrutchfield developed and produced the National Club Championship for Women, and the event is still going strong today. The event recognizes and celebrates the best women amateur club golfers from around the United States. It was a natural for Dinah Shore, considering her love of golf and down-to-earth personality, to be intricately involved. Dinah Shore graced the event with her presence and even received a lifetime achievement award from Fred Scrutchfield for her contributions to the growth of women's golf. (Fred Scrutchfield attended the University of Oklahoma on a golf scholarship. The passion has stayed with him for life.)

Today, Fred's company, SCI Sports and Entertainment Marketing of Nashville, Tennessee, produces a multitude of events. For example, for three years straight, Fred produced the Rolls Royce Series. Over fourteen days at various major markets, professional golfer Tom Kite provided lessons and golfed with thirty-six current owners and potential owners of these high-end automobiles. Rolls Royce dealers literally moved their showrooms out to the golf courses for test drives and show-and-tells. For Fred, event marketing is all about building relationships. "You need to assemble the right people with the right occasion: unique and memorable experiences are tremendous relationship and business-building tools."

Many of Fred Scrutchfield's events today combine golf, a private concert, and intimate cocktail receptions. Attendees and participants include business executives (and their clients), professional football players, professional baseball players, NASCAR drivers, politicians, comedians, country-music singers, popular artists, and community leaders. Why such a broad mix of celebrities? "Place ten people in a room and you'll get ten different definitions of a celebrity. Diversity is the key," says Fred. The end result is a tremendous environment where Impact Players from business get to know each other and often times begin to establish business relationships. Moreover, most of these events support a local or national charity. When Fred produces an event, everyone wins.

According to Fred, "It's not unusual for half of the attending Impact Players to work together in some fashion after one of these events. You can't underestimate the power of an informal setting. People have a tendency to open up and share ideas. If you have a customer or two with you at these events the opportunity for everyone to see people for who they are offers a tremendous platform to solve business issues and build new business opportunities."

At one of SCI's events, a large tire manufacturer brought in their distributors and wholesalers from Mexico to enhance the professional and personal bond between the organizations. At their table was world-class racecar driver and an Indy-500 winner Tom Sneva. Over a beverage, Tom Sneva talked about eclipsing the 200-mph mark. Fred Scrutchfield is adamant about event marketing and says, "You can bet that this shared experience brought everyone closer together. Event marketing bridges all types of gaps, even cultural ones. You don't see that type of relationship-building in the boardroom."

As the Information Age continues to mature, Fred believes that relationship-building through one-on-one experiences at event marketing venues will increase dramatically in importance. "In today's world, so much time is wasted due to phone tag, email overload, and lack of meaningful relationships. When you develop a relationship with your customers, on a one-on-one basis at unique events, people will make themselves available to you."

The Waring blender approach to business: golf, music, and entertainment has developed thousands of relationships and added millions of dollars to the bottom-line of Fred's business participants. Mixing business with pleasure just may be the recipe that your company needs to become an Impact Player in your industry. Just ask Fred Scrutchfield, the man who orchestrates it all.

Rick Novak with American hero Buzz Aldrin

Rick Novak and the Art of Building
a Vibrant Network of Leaders

You can't live a perfect day without doing something for someone who will never be able to repay you.

—John Wooden

Recently, at a minor league baseball game in Dayton, Ohio, I saw the power of networking. CEOs, CIOs, top military brass, entrepreneurs, educators, and civic leaders were all enjoying each other's company. A local businessman, Rick Novak, was throwing a retirement party for a senior officer from Wright Patterson Air Force base. Rick had worked his Rolodex to gather an impressive group of leaders.

The power of events like this and the way they change the course of life and the course of the world can't be overlooked or overestimated. It is events like this that foster business relationships, social relationships, and even marriages. The power of an introduction and shared experiences is the very fiber of our society. Impact Players like Rick Novak know that and have developed networking into an art. At the baseball game, I caught up with Rick and asked him a few questions about networking. First, let's get a quick glimpse of who Rick Novak is.

Richard Novak is a consultant who provides strategic planning, business development, and technology commercialization services. He has several graduate degrees. He was a Fulbright Scholar who studied in Germany, comparing U.S. and German information systems, technology, government, and educational collaborations focused on economic development.

His leadership responsibilities have included serving as co-chairperson of the Air Force Material Command (AFMC) Business Systems Summit, and previous service for four years as the Technology Workshops Committee chairperson for the Armed Forces Communications and Electronics Association (AFCEA) national InfoTech Conferences. Ohio Gov. Bob Taft appointed him to the Executive Order of the Ohio Commodore, which is committed to the economic development of Ohio from a global perspective.

Your network is especially strong in defense and government. Are these groups hard to network with?
The difficulties are the many barriers to entry. For example, many if not all of the military leaders, whom you need to access to discuss business development, live on the base at Wright Patterson Air Force Base. There is a "Catch-22": If you do not have a contract on base, you cannot be issued an ID. If you don't have an ID, then you can't get on base. Therefore, you can't do business with leaders on base.

Other difficulties entail turnover and rapidly-changing world conditions. For example, there is required movement of military and now civilian leaders—who are known as SESs," Senior Executive Service members—every one to four years to new responsibilities and typically new locations anywhere in the world. This forced turnover breaks the continuity of trust-building so crucial to new companies obtaining contracts with the Air Force.

Can you tell a story or two about how your network has helped people and organizations achieve success?
I convinced a reluctant vice president of an $800 million IT company to serve on a military conference committee. He not only established the trust he needed with a top government/military person, but it resulted in a $2 million contract, all without an ID to go on base.

How do you keep your network strong and vibrant?
Constant creative and fun activities focused on community-healthy activities, like this baseball game reception for 150 people, and serving on five boards of directors locally, as well as chairing four committees and serving on many more.

Ed Rigaud

Ed Rigaud: Obstacles Aren't True Impediments. They're Simply Part of the Landscape

Those who are free of resentful thoughts surely find peace.

—Buddha

Ed Rigaud's dream was to be an architect and follow in the footsteps of his hero, Frank Lloyd Wright. After all, to be an architect means you are able to use the whole brain, the creative side as well as the analytical.

For Ed, his dream could be realized at Louisiana State University. He grew up poor, but LSU was a school he could afford and one that was reputed to have an excellent architecture program. And it was a school he deserved to attend. He was a top student at his Catholic high school, St. Augustine in New Orleans. He had won numerous academic awards and graduated third in his class.

Ed's neighborhood was segregated except for the shops, whose proprietors were mostly Greeks and Italians. Ed Rigaud, an African-American, applied to LSU in 1961, only to receive a letter of rejection: Our policy won't allow you on campus.

Ed decided to attend Xavier University of New Orleans, which holds the distinction of being the only university that is Catholic and historically black. He would major in Chemistry, his best subject. When he graduated in 1965, Procter & Gamble was recruiting at Xavier. Ed knew the brands and was excited about the company. He accepted a job on the spot.

Ed has a passion for "the whole-brain thing." At Procter & Gamble, that meant switching from R&D to marketing and general management. It was a great transition for him and the company. Now Ed could manage the innovation process. He would establish a vision, model the process, and execute that vision. Eventually, Ed became general manager and vice president for several of P&G's food-and-beverage products.

In 1996, while at Procter & Gamble, Ed was on the board of the National Conference of Christians and Jews. Ed Rigaud would indeed get his chance to be an architect—an architect to build a bridge between races. John Pepper, then chairman and CEO of Procter & Gamble, chose him for the company's executive-on-loan program. Ed became executive director of the National Underground Railroad Freedom Center in Cincinnati. Two years became seven, and now Ed Rigaud is the permanent president of the center, an interactive education-and-research institution which is slated to open next year.

Ed talks about the mission and the need for the National Underground Railroad Freedom Center. His skills of analysis and synthesis have constantly been used for development of this national treasure. He relates its development to his model of the innovation process. First, leaders in the community *conceptualized* the Freedom Center. Those who conceptualized the center saw the consumer benefit and the need in the marketplace, and they helped integrate ideas on how to make the dream a reality. Second, the Freedom Center incorporated *modeling* to help people grasp the vision with a physical representation. Third came the *feasibility* of the Freedom Center, a step that included prototyping. Step four occurs when the actual *product* is introduced successfully.

Ed is excited about the Freedom Center and sees it as a way for people to learn the history of the Underground Railroad, a network of South-to-North routes and safe houses for people escaping slavery in the mid-1800s. The Freedom Center gives Americans a platform to tackle the psychological disease of racism. The Freedom Center addresses the root of the problem: slavery and America's unwillingness to discuss it. The Freedom Center speaks of hope and inspiration.

Ed emphasizes the positive. Where have people of different races worked together in a positive way? He points to the self-determination of the slaves who escaped and the abolitionists who risked their lives to help them. The National Underground Railroad Freedom Center is meant to be inspirational. Ed says it will:

1)   Build awareness of history and how it connects to today.

2)   Establish a dialogue empowering people to become facilitators of justice.

3)   Promote action resulting in increased community involvement.

4)   Facilitate the interaction of community leaders, benefiting all of society.

When you visit The National Underground Railroad Freedom Center and meet Ed Rigaud, you'll want to be part of the new landscape he is painting, a landscape that focuses on helping all people reach their full potential despite whatever obstacles they may face.

Edwin Rigaud's biography

Positions held

2003   *President, National Underground Railroad Freedom Center (Effective November 2001)*

2001   *President & CEO, National Underground Railroad Freedom Center (Retired from Procter & Gamble July 2001)*

1998   *President & CEO, National Underground Railroad Freedom Center (Executive on loan from Procter & Gamble)*

1996   *Executive Director, National Underground Railroad Freedom Center (Executive on loan from Procter & Gamble)*

1996   *Vice president, government relations, Procter & Gamble, North America*

1994   *Vice president, food-and-beverage products, Procter & Gamble, USA*

1992   *Vice president and general manager, food-and-beverage products, Commercial Service Products Group, Procter & Gamble, USA*

1991   *General manager, food-and-beverage products, Commercial Service Products Group, Procter & Gamble, USA*

Current local and national activities

Member, National Museum Services Board, Institute of Museum and Library Sciences (appointed by President Bush in 2002)

Member, Ohio Board of Regents (appointed by Gov. Bob Taft in 2002)

Member, Board of Directors, NextGen Corp., Cincinnati

Member, Board of Directors, Gamebanc, Colley Corporation, Cincinnati.

Member, CincinnatiCAN, Media, Communications, and Cultural Change Committee

Member, Junior League of Cincinnati Advisory Council

Member, Board of Trustees, Xavier University, Cincinnati, Ohio

Trustee Emeritus, National Conference for Community and Justice

Leadership Committee, Metropolitan Growth Alliance of Greater Cincinnati

Member, Ohio River Corridor Committee

Member, Board of Directors, Queen City Club, Cincinnati

Member, Board of Directors, Metropolitan Club, Covington, Kentucky

Trustee, Northern Kentucky Chamber of Commerce

Trustee, Xavier University of Louisiana

Awards:

Olympic Torchbearer, Salt Lake 2002 Winter Olympics Relay

YMCA Black Achiever Award, 1980

Lighthouse "On the Shoulders of Giants" Inaugural Award

Upscale Magazine "Top Power Brokers"

Applause Image Makers Award, 1998

Cincinnati Bell Building Bridges Award, 1998

Greater Cincinnati Convention and Visitors Bureau Annual Metropolitan Club Award for community Service, with wife, Carole Rigaud, 1998

The St. Thomas More Medallion, St. Thomas More College, 1998

Honorary doctorates from Northern Kentucky University and Mount St. Joseph College in Cincinnati

Doug MacMillan

Doug MacMillan: Plant Trees That You Will Never Sit Under

The best inheritance a parent can give his children is a few minutes of his time each day.

—Orlando A. Battista

September 11th. The date brings perspective to everyone's life. None more so than to Doug MacMillan, the best friend of Todd Beamer, who voiced those now heroic words "Let's Roll" on Flight 93. Not that Doug MacMillan needed a better perspective. For seven years before September 11th, Doug had had breakfast every Friday with a group of friends. Todd Beamer participated for four of those years. But these are no ordinary breakfast conversations.

These meetings are more like leadership roundtables. Each member of the group has a unique set of talents and they help each other grow. How? By focusing on the tenets of vulnerability and accountability. Every member can talk freely and emotionally about a weakness or trial and feel secure that it won't be discussed outside of the roundtable group. The group will offer advice for solving the problem. Then, in future meetings, each person is held accountable for the solution recommended to him.

It is through these breakfast meetings that Doug got to know Todd. He learned Todd's thinking on what a successful life entailed. To Todd, success meant forming in-depth relationships with family, friends, and customers and being there when they needed him most. In sales at Oracle, Todd thrived on working with the most difficult clients. He closed deals by forming personal relationships with them. Clients knew they could count on Todd. All Americans now know what Todd's family, friends, and clients already knew. All of us could count on Todd Beamer. Doug says, "Todd's default mode is what all of us saw on September 11th."

Since September 11th, there has been an organization and a person that traumatized children can count on. That organization is The Todd M. Beamer Foundation. The person is the foundation's CEO, Doug MacMillan. Doug believes The Todd Beamer Foundation is successful because 1) the focus is on the end user, the child suffering from trauma, and 2) the Foundation has surrounded itself with successful people. One of the key Impact Leaders supporting the Todd Beamer Foundation is Joe Gibbs, the former coach of the Washington Redskins and current owner of a NASCAR racing team. Doug is thankful that Coach Gibbs has adopted The Todd Beamer Foundation. "Coach Gibbs epitomizes the definition of success," Doug says. "He has helped the foundation immensely with his leadership skills."

I asked Doug if he defined success differently after September 11th. He said no. To him, success is still living in sync with his values. Those values haven't changed. What has changed is Doug's sense of urgency. His advice to all people is to use your talents and passion now, because time waits for no one. Doug heeded his own advice by taking a leadership role at the foundation. He now has the opportunity to honor his friend Todd's memory by combining his talents for public speaking and organizational leadership with his passion for helping others.

To reinforce the "value of time" message with everyone he meets, Doug uses a powerful medium. Doug has the watch that Todd wore on Flight 93. It is a constant reminder of the frailty of life. The watch reinforces the ultimate truth that time is our most valuable commodity. He suggests we spend it as Todd did, building strong relationships with one another.

For The Todd Beamer Foundation, success is the creation of resilient children. The foundation wants to create a generation of children who, when they are adults, help other traumatized children. One person helps ten. Then each of those ten helps ten others.

You've seen streets that are perfectly lined with 100-year-old old trees. Someone planted those trees knowing that subsequent generations would be the beneficiaries. The Todd M. Beamer Foundation and Doug MacMillan are planting trees of "hope" around the world. The fruit of their work is a new generation of "tree planters" who focus on building in-depth relationships with vulnerable children. Because of the foundation and Doug's work, children not even born yet will be able to sit under these trees of hope and be comforted. The message is clear: Successful people and successful organizations help others reach their full potential.

Sally Stewart

Sally Stewart Discovers Her Impact Niche
by Knowing What She Doesn't Like

Sally Stewart had reached the pinnacle of her career. As a seasoned journalist and chief West Coast correspondent for *USA TODAY*, Sally covered the O. J. Simpson murder trial, the San Francisco earthquake, the Los Angeles riots, and national politics. She moved on to excel in public relations as a vice president of both Edelman Public Relations and APCO Worldwide.

Anyone would call her successful. But Sally knew something was missing. She was looking for her Impact Niche. To help her discover her Impact Niche, Sally first developed a list of things she didn't like. The top three items on that list: 1) Working within the bureaucracy of a large consulting firm; 2) Enduring the standard morning and evening commute; and 3) Not being able to select her clients.

Next, she wrote down her motivations. Sally is motivated by helping others, by being financially compensated for the value she brings to the marketplace, and by helping senior executives clearly communicate their vision to their employees and to a wider audience. Most of all, Sally is motivated by the ability to control her own destiny.

She took a giant step toward achieving that goal when she began writing her first book, *Media Training 101*, which is scheduled for publication in October 2003. *Media Training 101* is the first step-by-step communications guide for executives. It is based on techniques Sally developed during her career as a journalist and corporate consultant.

By understanding her motivations and recognizing what she didn't like, Sally's Impact Niche became obvious. She would open her own corporate communications firm. Sally enjoys working with people and companies that can benefit from improving their communications skills and public profile. Her orientation led her to develop the guiding principle for *Media Training 101*, which is "The Three Commitments for a Successful PR Campaign." This innovative approach works with established companies as well as start-ups.

The tenets:

1) To succeed in public relations, companies must be "committed to wearing a white hat." Sally says a company that wears a white hat has a CEO and executive committee that are genuinely interested in helping society as well as their bottom line. For example, a pharmaceutical company that has developed a drug to help cure a disease must stress the benefits to

society as well as the profit potential. The guiding mission of the company must be greater than just making money.

2)   Any company that wants to have a successful public relations campaign must have the commitment and support of the executive committee. Organizational leaders must give their time and input to ensure success. Superior public relations does not happen in a vacuum.

3)   The vision developed and presented by any organization must be clear and without spin. Facts must be used to reinforce any statements made by the organization.

As the owner of her own business, Sally is enjoying the fruits of independence. "As a reporter, you're at the mercy of the news," she says. "Your personal life doesn't matter. You just have to drop what you're doing and cover the story. But now that I have my own company, I understand what success really is. Success is the ability to control one's time, and that makes life fun. After all, if you're not having fun at work, no matter what your title or salary, what good is it?"

Sally Stewart's Biography

Before founding her consulting group, SA Stewart Communications, in 2003, Sally was a vice president at two major public-relations agencies, Edelman Public Relations and APCO Worldwide, where she led and supported numerous accounts, including SKECHERS USA and Jenny Craig, Inc. She secured positive news coverage for her clients, including stories published in and/or televised on Forbes, The New York Times, CNN, The Wall Street Journal, Investor's Business Daily, CNBC, The Today Show, Fox News Channel *and* Money *magazine.*

While covering the O. J. Simpson trial, she was a regular commentator for CNN and KFAN Minneapolis. She has been an opinion columnist for the Los Angeles Daily News, *a freelance reporter for the Canadian Broadcasting Company and a journalism teacher for the University of California, Los Angeles Extension Journalism Program. She provides senior counsel to clients in effectively communicating complex issues and business strategies to the media. Her first book,* Media Training 101, *is scheduled for publication in October 2003 by Wiley.*

Pat Manocchia

Pat Manocchia: How Exercise Impacts the Whole Being

Lack of activity destroys the good condition of every human being, while movement and methodical physical exercise save it and preserve it.

—Plato

Pat Manocchia wants to have an impact on everyone's quality of life. Health care accounts for 14% of the Gross National Product in the United States. One half of that 14% is directly related to weight-related health issues. Pat, owner of La Palestra Center for Preventative Medicine in New York City and former national fitness expert on ABC's *Good Morning America*, says the solution is to learn the process of addressing the whole being.

You can't separate the physiological from the emotional parts of life, Pat says. All aspects of our existence are interrelated. To be healthy mentally and physically, a person must have a purpose in life, and that purpose must be bigger than you. "When you contribute to someone else's life, it gives meaning to your life," Pat says.

The body was meant to be used," Pat says. You have to establish a practice of taking care of yourself, and it starts with physical activity. Why? Because when you become active, physical, mental, and emotional changes occur. When a person exercises regularly, eating habits improve, the stress level goes down and the quality of sleep increases dramatically. The total person is rewarded by activity.

Even though Pat trains professional athletes from the NFL and NHL and other celebrities, he is firmly grounded on who his heroes are. The people he looks up to are those who contributed to his growth and gave him direction to help him achieve his sense of purpose, men of serious principle. These exceptional individuals include his father; John Rowe Workman, the late classics scholar at Brown University; and Bill Belisle, his high school hockey coach at Mount St. Charles. "Success in life is through service to others, and these are the people that served me and everyone else they came in contact with," Pat says.

Pat started La Palestra because he saw a huge gap between two massive industries, medicine and fitness. In his opinion, "Medicine folks don't particularly respect fitness guys, because people in medicine think all the fitness individuals are interested in are a good set of abs. Conversely, fitness experts think that people in medicine focus on a system that is backward in its approach—fix someone after the problem has occurred." He says both sides make valid points. But the real problem, in Pat's eyes, is the myth of two terms used every day: "preventive medicine" and "managed health care." Physical education in the United States is woeful and debunks the idea of preventive medicine. As for managed health care, the only thing managed is the cost, not the care.

To Pat, the answer is a multifaceted approach. First, participation must be emphasized over competition early in life. When kids get discouraged for whatever reason from joining sports in third grade, it can keep them from participating in sporting activities for the rest of their lives. Second, people must be educated to an ultimate truth: If you want to "Be like Mike," then put in the extra 400 hours of work per year that enabled Michael Jordan to excel at his sport.

The third thing Pat believes fully, like the Greeks, is that exercise allows you to explore your own limitations and abilities, which once learned can then be challenged and improved: "*mens sana in corporae sano*," sound mind in a sound body. Through physical discipline, people can develop mental and moral character (J. R. Workman).

Pat is emphatic: "Success in exercise, business, or life is the satisfaction that one intrinsically feels after dedication, perseverance, and hard work. It's the work, not the reward, that makes a person feel successful."

Dr. Kevin Elko

Dr. Kevin Elko: Build a Winning Season in Business

What do Pioneer Investments, the Dallas Cowboys, Abbott Diagnostics, The Pittsburgh Steelers, SmithKline Beecham, the University of Miami football team, Travelers Insurance Company, and the Cleveland Browns have in common? They use the services of Dr. Kevin Elko to build a winning season. A winning season in business? Yes, businesses that focus on a winning season maximize performance and morale. The key words are *winning* and *season*.

Winning

Dr. Elko believes that most people live lives of quiet desperation. They live life for the middle ground. Unfortunately, they're misguided, because life is not about being in the middle. What makes life worth living are the highs and the lows—the winning and the losing and the emotions that go along with winning and losing.

For many people, their favorite sports teams provide them with a substitute for their need to feel the highs and lows of life. Businesses have a real opportunity to maximize productivity by making winning and losing a part of life on the job. Dr. Elko says businesses that focus on winning or losing as a team achieve remarkable results. Businesses that do that are fulfilling a basic human desire. At the end of every day, people need to say "Today we won" or "Today we lost." Winning and losing are the spices of life. Leaders in business need to establish and communicate that vision to the team.

Why do businesses that focus on winning as a team succeed? Because when a business develops true team chemistry, people are drawn to each other in a network of support. Success occurs when the team achieves its goals. Individual goals are gladly subordinated.

However, leaders of these business teams, just like leaders in sports teams, must have the trust of their players. Just as importantly, the players must trust one another. Trust is particularly important in the Impact Society as diversity in the workforce grows. For example, the Miami Hurricanes football teams are successful each year because of the trust that exists on a team of Muslims, Cubans, Canadians, whites, and African-Americans, from both urban and rural backgrounds.

In successful organizations, trust is contagious. Leaders win over players, usually a small group at a time, and then those players win over other players, and so on.

Season

Great things happen when a business strives for a winning season, Dr. Elko says. A season has a beginning and an end. For a business, the season can mean a project. A project has a beginning and an end. People excel in an environment that is project-oriented as long as the project is time-sensitive with a clearly-defined mission. Dr. Elko recommends four seasons a year for a business—four definitive projects. A project requires a well-defined process and should outline the steps necessary to achieve success. The project has to be measurable. A scoreboard measures success along the way. Either you're winning or losing at your project. If you're winning, keep doing the things necessary to keep winning. If you're losing, assess the performance of the players and leaders alike. Adjustments to the process may have to be made.

In sports, a project could be winning a team's division or league. The process to win that division includes preparation, strategy, and ultimately celebration upon completion of the project. A winning season in business follows the same steps. And please don't forget the celebration part! People are motivated by rewards after a difficult project.

Dr. Elko says the most important tenet in developing a winning season is finding a way to bring all people on the team together, establishing a feeling of closeness. In life, a crisis pulls a group together. In the aftermath of September 11th, people didn't think of themselves as black or white, blue-collar or white-collar, rich or poor. Everyone was an American and everyone was on the same team. Unfortunately, in time, that closeness fades and is ultimately lost until another crisis emerges. In sports, a team can be pulled together by an us-against-them mentality. "Nobody thinks we can win; we'll show them!" In business, that closeness also has to be reached to achieve dramatic results. Forging that closeness is the job of the company's leadership. To excel, people in an organization need to feel the bond of trust and integrity that exists on a championship sports team.

Above all, if there's one thing to remember in building a winning season, Dr. Elko says, it's this: "Foster an environment of caring and love, because all human beings are wired for helping others."

Dick Wilson

Dick Wilson: Building a Diverse Network by Helping Others

It is one of the most beautiful compensations of this life that no man can sincerely try to help another without helping himself.
—Ralph Waldo Emerson, poet and philosopher

When you walk into Dick Wilson's office, it's obvious that this man enjoys meeting people. Pictures of Dick with world leaders, such as Muhammad Ali, are proudly displayed. When you talk to him, it's also obvious that Dick really enjoys helping people. By combining these two strengths, Dick has established a professional and personal network second to none.

Dick Wilson is a senior vice president of investments at a national financial institution. More than that, he is an Impact Player. His philosophy: "Whatever you do, do it with passion. Give everything you do 110%. If you're honestly wrong, it's not going to matter one way or another in a hundred years. It's better to take action and be wrong than take no action at all."

Dick is a humble man when talking about the extensive network that has enabled him to become a top earner in finance. He talks about keeping the peas and carrots in his life separate—a metaphor for the distinction between business and community work. You'll never find Dick with a business card when he is serving the community; he's just more comfortable operating that way.

Dick is a community leader. He is president of the Dream Factory (an organization that makes the wishes of ill children become reality) and founder of the Robinhood Project, which distributes the excess resources of corporate Louisville to homeless shelters. He has established a mentorship program at the University of Louisville where juniors and seniors meet doctors, lawyers, business people, and engineers to get a better understanding of the world awaiting them when they graduate.

As for business networking, Dick has established an event called The Breakfast of Champions, where community leaders work on their leadership skills at early-morning programs. This group of highly-motivated goal-setters has an estimated membership of over 750 Impact Players. It's not unusual for Dick to hold special engagements of high-profile speakers.

How extensive is Dick's network? He has a client base of over 3,500 successful people. He makes and takes between 100 and 150 phone calls daily, and his clients receive handwritten notes from him every six weeks. His office has three primary phone lines, including a hotline that he promises to answer in one ring for his best customers. All phone calls are returned the same day.

"Building a network of diverse Impact Players is the only way to reach your potential as a person," Dick says. "It's hard work, but it's a labor of love."

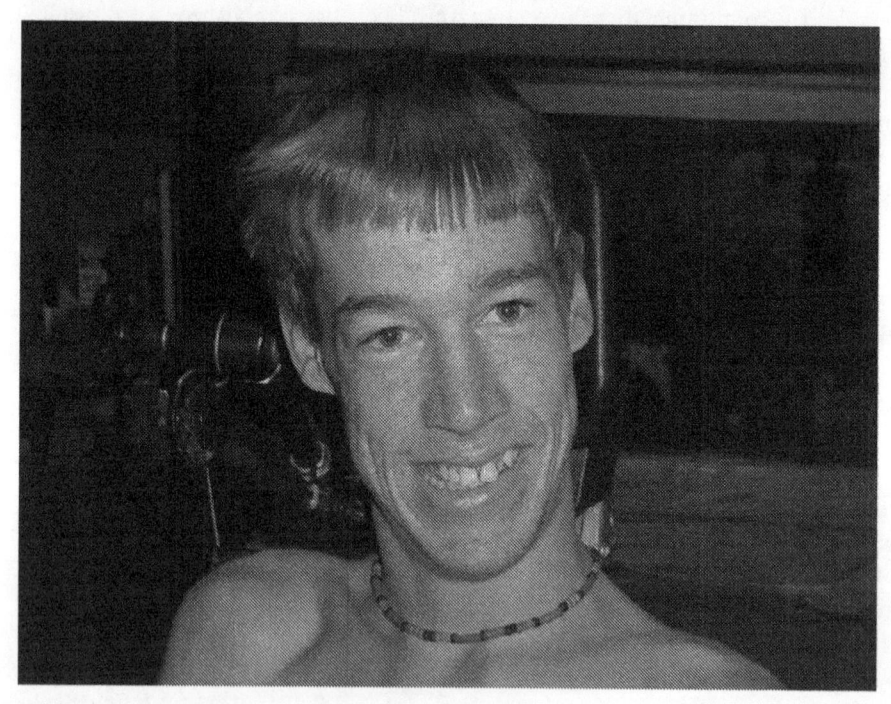

Brendan McPhillips

A Very Special Impact Player: Brendan McPhillips

Hope is a strange invention
A Patent of the Heart
In unremitting action
Yet never wearing out.

—Emily Dickinson

Brendan McPhillips meets me with an ear-to-ear grin. His computer-synthesized voice says, "Hi, Dick, it's great to see you again." It's been three long years since I saw Brendan last.

He shows me the PowerPoint presentations he has worked on diligently over the past six months. They're exceptional. Brendan does everything with a click of a mouse, but because he has cerebral palsy, a click of the mouse requires significant effort. The cursor moves when his head presses against a specially designed device that works with a software program. The computer and software are Brendan's connection to the outside world.

Brendan Patrick McPhillips is the greatest Impact Player I know. Now twenty-one years old, Brendan has raised money for charities, participated in marathons, and traveled extensively. His message is one of hope. Brendan's Impact Niche is that of a role model. Brendan gives hope to all people, and especially those with special challenges. He is front and center on the stage of persistence, resilience, dedication, discipline, and service to others. Those are all obvious Impact Player traits.

Brendan Patrick McPhillips was born on June 26, 1982, to Patrick McPhillips and Colleen Gilligan McPhillips. It was a difficult delivery, and it was soon discovered that Brendan had cerebral palsy. At six months, his schooling and therapy began at a children's hospital.

At four, he had an operation on his legs. Doctors clipped the muscles to give him better mobility. He attended Roselawn Condon, Stewart Elementary, and Princeton High School, and he is currently attending Scarlet Oaks, where he is developing his skills on Microsoft Office products.

Brendan enjoys professional football and is a friend of former Cincinnati Bengal kicker Doug Pelfrey. I first met Brendan at a charity golf event Doug was holding, a charity that has supported Brendan's needs.

Pushed in his wheelchair, Brendan participates in marathons to raise money for children with leukemia. He and his mom, who passed away from a heart attack at forty-two on December 30, 1999, raised a great deal of money and attention for the leukemia foundation. He has completed marathons in Bermuda, Hawaii, and Ireland. He participated in a Chicago marathon, where he was spotted and sponsored by Nike. His favorite city is San Diego. Brendan loves to travel, go to concerts, camp, and hang out with his family.

In 1998, Brendan had a pump put into his abdomen that releases medication automatically into his system. This has helped him to better control his spastic movement. He has his pump filled every few weeks. He has receives homecare twenty-four hours a day, except when he spends the weekend with his aunt and uncle.

Brendan has a great sense of humor and an unshakeable faith in God. He tends to touch people one way or another when he meets them. To see him smile or laugh is very special. Brendan is very empathetic and sensitive to others and he is never without a smile. His goal is to spread hope to those who don't have any. He lives life to the max every day.

His discipline is greater than that of any professional athlete.
His persistence is greater than that of any entrepreneur.
His success is greater than the achievement of the wealthiest businessperson.
His wisdom is greater than the knowledge of any scholar.
His belief in God is as great as the faith of any person of the cloth.
His legacy will be unattainable for most of us.

May we learn from Brendan McPhillips and other challenged people. Their example is a shining star on the path to becoming an Impact Player.

Lessons in Leadership

Impact Leaders

Formulate and stamp indelibly on your mind a mental picture of yourself as succeeding. Hold this picture tenaciously. Never permit it to fade. Your mind will seek to develop the picture...Do not build up obstacles in your imagination.

—**Norman Vincent Peale, minister and leader in positive thinking**

Impact Leaders are Impact Players who are in positions of leadership. Impact Leaders understand, appreciate, empower, and serve people, which motivates everyone around them to achieve the Impact Leader's consistent and clearly-articulated organizational focus of positively shaping the Impact Society.

Impact Leaders are reality visionaries who clearly, consistently, and constantly communicate their vision to everyone in their organization. Impact Leaders know what the Impact Niche is for each Impact Player in their organization. They know what their Impact Players are good at and help them refine their skills.

Leaders Empower

The best leader is one who has sense enough to pick good people to do what needs to be done, and self-restraint enough to keep from meddling with them while they do it.

—**President Theodore Roosevelt**

The picture of leadership in the Impact Society is clear when you listen to the Impact Leaders. They stress that today's innovative organizations are built around leadership, not management.

Manage knowledge.
Manage information.
Lead people.

Impact Leaders and Orientation

As a rule, he who has the most information will have the greatest success in life.
—Benjamin Disraeli, nineteenth-century British prime minister

Orientation is a person's unique recipe for perspective, consisting of experiences, biases, education, interrelationships, and current situational analysis. Want to make better decisions? Impact Leaders understand that they must constantly expand their orientation.

Impact Leaders want different perspectives to enhance their personal orientation, vision, and decision-making skills. Impact Leaders want to know the lifestyles and thoughts of old, young, black, white, men, women, physically-challenged, professionals, and blue-collar workers. Impact Leaders understand others before trying to be understood.

Impact Leaders Emphasize Hiring the Right People

Never tell people how to do things. Tell them what to do and they'll surprise you with their ingenuity.
—Gen. George S. Patton

Organizations that emphasize leadership surround their Impact Leaders with Impact Players, because those are the people who make a real difference. Successful organizations hire the most talented, motivated people and place them in the right jobs.

Impact Leaders Don't Manage, They Lead

Lead: to show the way by going in advance; conduct; escort; direct.
Manage: to exert control over; make submissive to one's authority, discipline, or persuasion.
—American Heritage Dictionary of the English Language

There's no need to manage Impact Players, because they know what has to be done and they have the knowledge, motivation, and skill set to do it. It is the job of Impact Leaders to empower Impact Players to carry out their jobs by giving them a clear understanding of how they are helping to achieve the ultimate objective of the organization. Lead Impact Players—don't manage them!

Unfortunately, many organizations today implement a "command-and-control" style of management. This inefficient model results in low morale, high turnover, and little or no creativity or innovation. Whether they know it or not, command-and-control organizations are positioning themselves for failure. The value of Impact Players is their specialized know-how, their Impact Niche. If you act as their boss instead of their partner, they'll go elsewhere. When intellectual capital leaves, it's not easily replaceable. Even harder to replace is the Impact Player's focus on results.

The first question an organization should ask is, "Do we want to manage people or lead them?" To use a sports analogy, Impact Leaders are like good coaches. They prepare their team and then they let the players play.

Impact Leaders Serve Others

To lead people, walk beside them…As for the best leaders, the people do not notice their existence. The next best, the people honor and praise. The next, the people fear; and the next, the people hate…When the best leader's work is done, the people say, 'We did it ourselves!'

—Lao-tsu, philosopher

Impact Leaders would never ask someone to do something that they would not do themselves. Impact Leaders build people up. They despise people who tear others down.

Impact Leaders understand that they must invest in the minds of their people. The greatest asset any organization has is its people, and that asset must be continually upgraded through education and training.

Impact Leaders Emphasize Stability

Leadership and learning are indispensable to each other.

—President John F. Kennedy

Impact Leaders understand that people in their organization need stability, especially after September 11th. This does not mean lifetime employment. It means a well-thought-out program of continuing education for each employee/partner that includes on-the-job training, classroom work, and innovation training.

Impact Leaders Embrace Change

Where there is no vision, the people perish.

—Proverbs (29:18)

Impact Leaders know the dichotomy of the Impact Economy: organizations that excel at adapting to change are more stable. *Impact Leaders have the vision to question all assumptions and attempt to see all obstacles ahead.* By doing those two things, organizations can be better prepared and therefore more stable.

Impact Leaders Establish a Covenant

In order to be a leader, a man must have followers. And to have followers, a man must have their confidence. Hence, the supreme quality for a leader is unquestionably integrity. Without it, no real success is possible, no matter whether it is on a section gang, a football field, in an army, or in an office. If a man's associates find him guilty of being phony, if they find that he lacks forthright integrity, he will fail. His teachings and actions must square with each other. The first great need, therefore, is integrity and high purpose.

—President Dwight D. Eisenhower

Impact Leaders must establish a covenant with all stakeholders (employees, suppliers, shareholders, community). A covenant with shareholders alone led to the decay of leadership in our major corporations. As a result, faith in our capitalistic system diminished and laws were enacted that reduced every business owners' liberties. True Impact Leaders of corporations understand that they must balance commitments to the individual, society, and shareholders to succeed.

Impact Leaders Appreciate Entrepreneurship

Entrepreneurs are the forgotten heroes of America.

—Ronald Reagan

Impact Leaders realize that the Impact Economy is powered by entrepreneurial thinking.

Entrepreneurial businesses are having a significant impact on the economy. In Kansas City, 111% of net new jobs were created by companies less than five years old and with less than twenty-five employees.

—Kurt Mueller, senior vice president, The Kauffman Foundation

Kurt Mueller says women and minorities are leading the way in establishing successful businesses. Mueller wants to see entrepreneurial studies in grade school education. The Kauffman Foundation estimates that 33% of children entering kindergarten display entrepreneurial skill sets, but by their senior year in high school, the schools' conformity approach has whittled that number down to a sad 3%.

Impact Leaders Attract and Retain Impact Players

Whatever you choose for yourself, give to another. If you choose to be happy, cause another to be happy. If you choose to be prosperous, cause another to prosper. If you choose more love in your life, cause another to have more love in theirs.

—*Conversations with God (Book 3)*, through Neale Donald Walsch

One of the most important jobs of Impact Leaders is attracting and retaining Impact Players for their organizations. How is this accomplished? To begin: 1) Hire the right people. 2) Place them in the right positions. 3) Understand what motivates them. Impact Leaders use written assessment tools to hire Impact Players. These assessment tools predict performance. They measure talent. They measure motivation. If they have the talent to excel at the job, do they have the motivation to do so? If so, what motivates them?

Impact Leaders: How Impact Players Lead

Coach Marvin Lewis

Impact Leader Coach Marvin Lewis:
"Conceive, Believe, Achieve"

A major transformation is underway in Cincinnati. The Cincinnati Bengals have an Impact Leader at the helm. Coach Marvin Lewis is the picture of an Impact Leader that demands Continuous Performance Improvement.

> *The ultimate role of a leader is to develop a clear vision for your organiza-*
> *tion, to have the diligence and passion to see it through and the communi-*
> *cation skills to draw people together in order to achieve a common goal.*
>
> **—Marvin Lewis**

Here's a prediction, and please hold me to it: The Cincinnati Bengals will win a Super Bowl within four years. There will be doubters in the beginning, the first year or two won't be easy and the team will incur many losses because change takes time, but he will succeed. Here are my five reasons for this prediction.

1) Marvin Lewis is building a culture of people first. He met everyone in the Bengals' organization in his first week there (a first by a coach or anyone else in team history).

2) Marvin Lewis is building a culture of discipline., not through excessive controls but through thoroughness. It may take time, but the attribute of "thoroughness" will permeate every player on that team. No one will outwork Marvin Lewis or his organization. No one will possess more knowledge on game day than Marvin Lewis and his team. No one will be better prepared than the Cincinnati Bengals. Marvin Lewis is the definition of discipline, and he is surrounding himself with disciplined people.

3) Marvin Lewis has a vision and a plan for that vision, which is relentless. Furthermore, he constantly communicates that vision to everyone in the organization. He knows where his team is going—to the Super Bowl— and his team will display a consistent effort to get there. You won't see a major overhaul once Marvin Lewis gets his system in place. Rather, you'll see purposeful readjustments and incremental realignments. Slow and steady. Adjust. Slow and steady. Adjust. Slow and steady. Championship!

4) Marvin Lewis is an Impact Player. He is not afraid to shoulder the responsibility to make the big play. He has prepared himself as well as anyone to be a head coach in the National Football League. The position he is in now is a result of his life's work. The natural result of that preparation will be a world championship.

5)　Marvin Lewis will give credit to the team and the organization when they win and will stand front and center when they lose. Players will play for him.

Coach Lewis has a favorite saying that anyone in a position of leadership should remember. "All of us are smarter than any one of us." It's obvious talking with Coach Lewis that he believes two-way communication is one of the keys to being successful. He surrounds himself with assistant coaches who aspire to move up the coaching ladder and who hold similar beliefs and share the same passion. He values group input but he knows that the ultimate decision rests with the Impact Leader. Coach Lewis values diversity and the fresh ideas that diversity brings. After all, there is no one right way to do something.

Asked about the challenges of being a coach in the NFL, Lewis says you spend a lot of time with people who know the outcome they want but don't understand the little steps necessary to reach it. Reaching that outcome, a world championship, is more of an art than a science, he says. Coach Lewis has a quiet determination and resolve to do whatever is necessary to produce a winner.

Marvin Lewis wants to surround himself with Impact Players. He does that by observing interaction and observing ability. He goes back to where an athlete went to college. He wants to know how the players interacted with trainers, other players, and students. How does the athlete react after a good or a bad play? What is his character? Then Coach Lewis watches tapes to observe ability. How does the player perform on the field? In the end, it's a 50/50 grading system: talent and character.

Coach Lewis is an Impact Leader because he not only does things right but he does the right things.

Marvin Lewis' Biography

Before joining the Cincinnati Bengals as head coach, Marvin Lewis directed the NFL's fifth-ranked defensive unit in Washington in 2002, serving as assistant head coach in addition to his coordinator's role. He went to the Redskins after six seasons as defensive coordinator with the Baltimore Ravens, a tenure that included a Super Bowl victory following the 2000 season.

In the 2000 regular season, Lewis' Baltimore defense set the NFL record for fewest points allowed in a sixteen-game campaign (165), clipping twenty-two points off the previous mark. In total yardage allowed, Lewis' last three Baltimore defenses each ranked No. 2 in the NFL. His 2001 unit also led the Ravens to the league's second-fewest points allowed and finished in the top four in six other categories.

He began his coaching career working with the linebackers at his alma mater, Idaho State (1981–84). The Bengals finished 12-1 during Lewis' first season and won the NCAA Division 1-A championship.

Lewis received his bachelor's degree in Physical Education from Idaho State in 1981 and earned a master's in Athletic Administration in 1982. He was inducted into Idaho State's Hall of Fame in 2001. He and his wife, Peggy, have a daughter, Whitney, and a son, Marcus.

Active in his community, Lewis has been honored as "Assistant Coach of the Year" by the Pro Football Writers Association and was named "Man of the Year" in 2001 by The Washington (Pa.) Observer. In Baltimore, he was involved with numerous philanthropic groups, including the American Red Cross and Muscular Dystrophy of Baltimore. In 2002, he joined the Washington Redskins Leadership Council's Honorary Committee, assisting in community and youth outreach efforts of the organization throughout the D.C. area.

Dr. Lee Todd

Dr. Lee Todd: An Impact Leader Who Dreams

Success is advancing confidently in the direction of your own dreams.
—Henry David Thoreau

The ingredients of innovation and wealth creation are readily available at research universities. Certainly the sheer number of Impact Players at a research university is extraordinary. Sometimes, all that is missing is an Impact Leader to show them the way.

There are three things we noticed about Dr. Lee Todd, president of the University of Kentucky, when we interviewed him: his warmth, his intensity, and his sense of mission to positively impact society, the economy and the individual. His vision is to create a top-20 University, and in his words, "There is no room for slackers."

Dr. Todd has a very clear vision and communicates that vision exceptionally well. The result of his organizational focus is an institution that is benefiting society and its stakeholders. Dr. Todd is definitely an Impact Leader! He views the University of Kentucky as an institution that must fulfill responsibilities to society by making life healthier, to the economy by creating new jobs via innovation and commercialization, to itself by being self-sufficient, and to individuals by helping them achieve their dreams.

The Business of Innovation and Commercialization

Dr. Todd says universities need to become revenue generators, and the best way to do that is through innovation and commercialization. In the Impact Society, universities will look like holding companies. Revenue generation is well underway at the University of Kentucky. Here's how the university describes one of its initiatives.

"The Advanced Science and Technology Commercialization Center, better known as ASTeCC, is the University of Kentucky's nexus for multidisciplinary research that leads to technology transfer and new business start-ups. The ASTeCC program is a catalyst for the university's economic development mission, serving as a hub for faculty who want to license their technology and/or start a company.

"UK's Coldstream Research Campus also offers lab space and counts among its current tenant roster some businesses from ASTeCC that have 'graduated.'

"Not only does UK play a critical role in economic development, but it also has a tremendous impact on the state's economy each year. During last fiscal year alone, research grants and contracts from out-of-state sources resulted in a

$432.5-million-contribution to Kentucky's economy, including $138.6 million in personal income and 7,636 jobs, 5,759 of which are directly related to research (source: *IMPLAN Economic Impact Model*, UK Center for Business and Economic Research).

"The development, management, and transfer of the university's intellectual property generates new technology, products, and businesses, creates jobs that enable university graduates to stay in the Commonwealth, and enhances our quality of life."

Impact Leaders Dream

Impact Leaders have the ability to dream and articulate their dream into a clear vision for others to follow. Dr. Todd's inaugural speech captures the essence of this powerful Impact Player trait. The following is an excerpt from Dr. Todd's Inaugural Address.

A New Way to Dream

"I have chosen the title of my inaugural address to be 'A New Way to Dream.' The inspiration for this title came several years ago when Patsy (his wife) and I were standing in line to see *Sunset Boulevard* on Broadway. My mind was wandering because I had to return to Kentucky on Monday and give a major speech to a group of teachers, and I had not yet begun to write it. I told myself, "Forget about the speech, *enjoy the play*, worry about the speech later."

"As the play developed, the car of a young playwright, Joe Gillis, stalled in front of the mansion owned by Ms. Norma Desmond, an actress who had been a big star in the silent movies but who had not made the transition to the 'talkies.' In their conversation, Joe asked Ms. Desmond what it was like to be in the early movies. Her comment to him was, *"We gave the world new ways to dream,"* and then she launched into the beautiful song that Kathryn and our wonderful orchestra just performed.

"In the darkness of the theater, I whispered to Patsy, 'I just got the title of my speech.' I have used that title for several speeches I have given to teachers and students over the years. I talk about the fact that our heritage has not given us a good basis from which to dream. Our low self-esteem has limited our ability to dream of a world in which we can compete just like everyone else. I believe my theme, 'A New Way to Dream,' is timely because we are at a point in the state's history where those dreams can become realities.

"Dreams have always been important to me. I have been able to live out several of them. The results have *exceeded* what I could have ever imagined. I graduated from the University of Kentucky, married my childhood sweetheart, graduated from MIT, taught at the University of Kentucky, had two wonderful children, started two companies, *and now have the job of a lifetime!* While I have been able to live out these dreams, looking back I realize that I *never dreamed big enough.*

"For instance, I never allowed myself to dream that I would be the president of the University of Kentucky. In the last few months, I have spoken to over 5000 students, and I have challenged them to *dream big,* to *lift their vision fifteen degrees higher!* I tell them that they can go farther than they think they can go. They can go farther than they are being told they can go. They need a 'new way to dream.'

"As I began thinking about assuming this position, I sensed that this university was restless and needed to dream. That's why I left my job three months early, so I could meet with faculty and staff and ask them to tell me *their needs and their dreams.* I got the sense that while a few people had some dreams, others had been so discouraged that they had allowed their dreams to die. Their drive to dream had been lost.

"People who fail to dream do so because they *cannot believe* their dreams will ever result in reality. While we may not be able to implement everything, if we *don't believe we can dream,* we will greatly limit the potential of this institution.

"Dr. Thomas Clark, our mountain of wisdom, told me yesterday, 'An institution must be led by someone who dreams.'

"Anatole France, the French writer and winner of the Nobel Prize for literature, said, 'To accomplish great things, we must not only *act,* but also *dream*; not only *plan,* but also *believe.*'

"My advice to you: Unleash your dreams and let's work together to make them a reality. Let's begin 'a new way to dream'—to dream with the *belief* and the *expectation* that *together* we can make it happen!'"

Dr. Lee Todd's Resume

Dr. Todd officially began his term as UK's 11th president on July 1, 2001. Prior to his UK presidency, Dr. Todd was senior vice president of Lotus Development, where he led the Messaging and Collaboration Business Unit, one of three business units at Lotus. In this capacity, he was responsible for such traditional Lotus products as Notes, Domino, and SmartSuite. He oversaw collaborative offerings such as Sametime and QuickPlace.

Dr. Todd received his bachelor of science degree in Electrical Engineering from the University of Kentucky in 1968 and his master of Science and doctorate in Electrical Engineering from the Massachusetts Institute of Technology in 1970 and 1973, respectively. While a graduate student at MIT, he received six U.S. patents in high-resolution display technology. It was during that time that he began proposing the application of telecommunications and high-resolution displays for data conferencing.

Dr. Todd founded Projectron, Inc., in 1981 to manufacture projection cathode-ray tubes for the flight-simulation industry. The Projectron picture tube was used in approximately 90% of commercial flight simulators as well as numerous military simulators. In 1990, Projectron was sold to Hughes Aircraft Company. Dr. Todd convinced Hughes to move its CRT operations in California and New York to Kentucky. He worked with the University of Kentucky and government officials to start the University's Coldstream Research Campus with Hughes Display Products as the first tenant.

Dr. Todd incorporated DataBeam Corporation in 1976, but major financing and product development did not occur until 1983. DataBeam has been the world's leading provider of real-time collaboration and real-time distance-learning software and development platforms. Approximately 160 companies (including Cisco, Lucent, Microsoft, and AT&T) were licensees of DataBeam technology. Investors included individuals, venture capitalists, Intel, and Cisco Systems. Most of DataBeam's technical staff consisted of UK engineering and computer-science graduates. DataBeam was acquired by IBM in June of 1998 and now reports to Lotus Development Company, a subsidiary of IBM.

Bill Robinson

Bill Robinson: An Impact Leader Heading "Upward and Onward"

The greatest virtues are those which are most useful to other persons.

—Aristotle

Bill Robinson is an attorney who does more in one day than most people do in a week. As a member of the American Bar Association's Board of Governors, he has reached the pinnacle of success in his profession. The motto he lives by: "Upward and onward." His life is based on a concept he calls "otherness," which he defines as serving others by making a positive difference in their lives. He believes the opportunity to help others is always an opportunity to better oneself. Bill walks the talk. He has served in many civic and professional volunteer leadership roles, including:

- *Cincinnati/No. Ky. International Airport, board vice chair*
- *Kentucky Bar Association, fiftieth president*
- *Cincinnati Institute of Fine Arts, board member*
- *National Underground Railroad Freedom Center, advisory trustee*
- *Cincinnati Symphony Orchestra, board of trustees*
- *National Conference of Community & Justice, board co-chair*
- *Kentucky Chamber of Commerce, board chair*
- *United Way of Greater Cincinnati, board member*

Bill describes life as the Alpha and Omega of one's personal development on this Earth. Success occurs only by challenging oneself, and there's a lot more perspiration in success than inspiration.

His experience and success demonstrate that the careers of successful people have a clear continuity. Hard work, discipline, long hours, passion for excellence, high energy, self-awareness, and correct self-assessment, combined with clear vision, ultimately and repeatedly lead to success.

Bill views change as an opportunity for personal growth. When change is approached with a positive attitude, it can lead to a greater sense of personal and professional fulfillment. He often uses the word "attitude" and insists that attitude is frequently a distinguishing characteristic of those who repeatedly achieve success in the face of change.

Bill outlines the importance of innovation to a successful career. Innovation is simply a requirement for success. Problem-solving requires unique thinking. Innovation is the key to opening the door to solutions for clients. A very important tenet for professional success is a laser-like focus on the client's best interests in the solution of problems.

Bill defines an "Impact Player" as a person who brings to every challenge and opportunity a high level of emotional energy and commitment to excellence. The reaction of others to such intensity may be intimidating, interesting, or attractive, but there is always an "impact" causing a definite emotional and, often, intellectual reaction in others.

For example, Pete Rose was a warrior on the baseball field. If you were a Cincinnati Reds fan, you loved the aggressive way he played the game. On the other hand, if you were a fan of the opposing team, Pete Rose was typically the object of resentment and vilification. Either way, Pete had a definite impact.

As for Bill's view on how to succeed as a member in the Impact Economy, it's got to be "upward and onward," or it's not worth doing!

Building an Impact Organization: How to Attract and Retain Impact Players

Build an Impact-Player Organization

Imagine what a harmonious world it could be if every single person, both young and old, shared a little of what he is good at doing.

—Quincy Jones, musician

For organizations to survive and then thrive, they must practice Continuous Performance Improvement strategies to attract and retain the finest Impact Players. The reality that businesses and all organizations must wake up to is that the demand for top Impact Players is greater than the supply. The ratio will continually grow in favor of the all-star Impact Player. Gaining the ultimate competitive advantage depends on hiring a team of Impact Players.

Fifteen Steps to Keeping Impact Players

Here is how to attract and retain superior Impact Players.

1) Appreciate the work they do.
2) Pay them based on performance.
3) Empower them to make decisions.
4) Don't micromanage them.
5) Develop a clear organizational focus so Impact Players can see how their work fits into the big picture.
6) Develop an organizational focus that is good for the customer, individual, society, and financial health of the business.
7) Develop a well-thought-out plan of Continuous Performance Improvement, incorporating ongoing training and education.
8) Develop a consistent methodology for assessing and rewarding job performance.

9) Dismiss judgmental associates.

10) Develop a diverse group of associates.

11) Don't treat Impact Players as employees. Treat them as partners.

12) Be flexible.

13) Locate your company in a region with strong natural amenities, structural amenities, and social amenities.

14) Use an assessment tool to make sure you are hiring the right people to fill your positions.

15) Hire people who share the same vision as the corporation and are motivated by a sense of mission.

Let's view each step in a little more detail.

1) Appreciate the work Impact Players do.

Many companies seem to focus on the financial aspect of motivation. That overlooks the fact that people are wired to respond to acknowledgement of a job well done. Leaders of organizations must thank their Impact Players. Appreciating the work someone does costs nothing and increases performance and loyalty. A one-on-one appreciation session is a great way for a team leader to motivate an Impact Player.

2) Pay Impact Players based on performance.

Impact Players know their value in the marketplace, and today's world is too competitive not to pay them based on performance. Give Impact Players well-defined projects with well-defined goals and objectives. Make sure to divide a year into four seasons. Once a year is too infrequently to celebrate a win. Just as you would to an Impact Player in sports, pay them for meeting these goals and objectives. Why not? The whole organization benefits when they do.

3) Empower Impact Players to make decisions.

The era when corporate headquarters make all key decisions is quickly coming to an end. The world today needs quick and accurate decision-making skills from throughout a decentralized organization. Impact Players have the knowledge, confidence, and courage to make decisions, and they relish the opportunity to do so. Today's effective organizations think of themselves as knowledge networks, not power-holding silos. There's not enough bandwidth not to empower Impact Players to make decisions. Impact Players are motivated by being able to use their knowledge. Impact Player empowerment increases loyalty and the efficiency of an organization, and it costs little to implement.

4) Don't micromanage Impact Players.

Impact Players in business are like Impact Players in sports. They like to play. They have talent and the motivation needed to produce consistent high-end results. Why not let them use their skills? Micromanagement, extensive paperwork, and so on only frustrate Impact Players. Set goals for Impact Players that are achievable, flexible, measurable, and reviewable. In doing so, an organization keeps control of performance while minimizing management.

5) Develop a clear organizational focus so Impact Players can see how their work fits into the big picture.

When you ask Impact Players to sacrifice for the team and work long hours, they need to know why. Why should I give up time with my family? Why should I give up my Wednesday-night golf league? Why should I postpone my vacation for this project? First, Impact Players need to understand the vision of the company. Second, they need to know how their work helps the team. There are many positions within an organization that don't receive the glory, but if people see how their work helps the organization attain its organizational focus, then they will be satisfied. In football, the goal is to score more points than the opponent. Each position player has a role to play in that organizational focus. Successful coaches constantly communicate the organizational focus. As a matter of fact, it is one of their most important jobs. Leaders in business and other organizations should constantly do the same. One of a leader's key tasks should be to continually communicate the organizational focus and how everyone has a role to play.

6) Develop an organizational focus that is good for the shareholders, customers, individuals, society, and financial health of the business.

Historically, in the United States, the organizational focus has been on the shareholder. In Japan, the organizational focus is on the worker in the form of lifetime employment. In Europe, the organizational focus is on society. It's time for businesses to balance the organizational focus on the needs of shareholders, workers, vendors, community, and society as a whole. The short-term focus on shareholder value has led to the lack of trust in corporate America today. Good business cannot be placed in silos. Good business means rewarding shareholders with a good return on investment. Good business means providing workers with the financial stability they need to work hard and enjoy life. Good business means dealing with vendors to develop a symbiotic, cooperative relationship. Good business means giving back to society. Impact Players want to work for companies that understand and implement these values.

7) Develop a well-thought-out plan of Continuous Performance Improvement incorporating ongoing training and education.

Impact Players value functional education. They realize their value in the marketplace is directly related to education and experience. To retain Impact Players, show them the training and education they are going to receive and how this education will impact their lives. Place an education-and-training personal development plan in their file. Make sure it is implemented in a consistent and timely fashion. Education breeds productivity and loyalty.

8) Develop a consistent methodology for assessing and rewarding job performance.

Impact Players relish consistent and fair job assessments. Impact Players like setting goals, reaching their goals and being challenged. The methodology must be consistent and fair. A hierarchy where career advancement can be sabotaged by one person must be replaced by an objective system. Impact Players place a high value on being treated fairly. A consistent evaluation process should focus on results. After all, superior Impact Players focus on getting the job done and done well. For an organization, the benefits of developing a consistent job performance assessment system go right to the bottom line.

9) Dismiss judgmental associates.

Impact Players like to discover, innovate and produce new and better ways of doing things. These traits are exactly what a thriving organization looks for. When an organization has judgmental associates, creativity and innovation are thwarted. Impact Players stymied by judgmental organizations will leave. If you want to create wealth via innovation, get rid of judgmental associates.

10) Incorporate a diverse group of associates.

Impact Players enjoy broadening their orientation, and orientation can be greatly increased by the transfer of knowledge within a group. The more diverse the group, the more expansive the knowledge. With better knowledge, Impact Players can make better decisions. Better decisions mean better profits. If you're a consumer-goods company trying to gain market share in the U.S. Hispanic marketplace, wouldn't it be better to have someone on your marketing committee who understands that marketplace?

11) Don't treat Impact Players as employees. Treat them as partners.

Impact Players have the knowledge, expertise, and motivation needed to drive profits. Impact Players are the difference. They know this and expect to be treated as equals. They enjoy being on a team and understand that a team needs all positions to be filled by the best players in order to maximize productivity. Command-and-control style leadership will reduce performance and ultimately drive Impact Players away. "Appreciate-and-empower" is the leadership style that allows Impact Players to thrive.

12) Be flexible.

We live in a connected world. Many Impact Players are parents and may want to work at home from time to time to be with their children. Let them. Impact Players pride themselves on having their priorities in order. Especially after September 11th, family and work must be in balance for this group. Demographics are changing. More and more women than ever are in positions of leadership. Technology has enabled us to be always connected. Be flexible and let Impact Players perform their jobs in new and creative environments. Watch the Impact-Player labor pool explode when you approach the market with a creative way to address an ever-changing world.

13) Locate your company in a region with strong natural amenities (parks), structural amenities (good schools), and social amenities (diverse population).

Impact Players are always looking to improve their quality of life. When deciding where to open an office, consider what the area has to offer. Demanding morning and evening commutes are draining many of the best minds away from the traditional big power centers. Provide value to Impact Players by surrounding them with what they want. This strategy alone is paying off for some of the smartest companies.

14) Use an assessment tool to make sure you are hiring the right people to fill your positions.

Anyone can be an Impact Player in the right position. All too often, an interview and an impressive resume are all it takes for some companies to make a hiring decision. When you're hiring for a specific job, assess a candidate for the talents and motivations needed to perform that job at a consistently high level. A star performer in sales is often rewarded with a sales management position. The skill set needed for sales and the skill set needed for management can be diametrically opposed. As the saying goes, all a company does is lose a good salesperson and gain a bad sales manager. Besides, talent assessment tools can also measure motivation.

What good is it to hire a person who has all the talent in the world but lacks motivation? Impact Players succeed when their skills and motivations match the positions they are hired to fill. The Continuous Performance Improvement of your organization depends on a quality predictive-assessment instrument.

15) Hire people who share the same vision as the corporation and are motivated by a sense of mission.

Impact Players love to be part of a team. Those who share the same vision and sense of mission as the team will be extremely loyal, even when the competition tries to hire them away for a few more dollars. If you want your organization to be populated with high-level Impact Players, communicate the organization's mission and see if they are driven by that sense of mission. Use a professional assessment tool to predict what the player can and will accomplish.

The Impact Leader Challenge™

True leadership is the art of changing a group from what it is to what it ought to be.

—Virginia Allan, stateswoman

Are you ready to take the Impact Leader Challenge and lead your organization to an exciting new level of performance? If you don't, who will?

Step 1—Impact Leader Defined

Write down the attributes of an Impact Leader (below) in your journal and on two index cards. One of the cards is for home and the other is for work. Please read them in the morning, at lunch, and at night.

I am an Impact Leader because I:

> ➤ Am a passionate reality visionary.
>
> ➤ Thrive on innovation and being an agent of change.
>
> ➤ Listen to a diverse group of individuals who give me a broader perspective, which allows me to make better and more well informed decisions.
>
> ➤ Clearly, consistently, and constantly communicate my vision.
>
> ➤ Understand, appreciate, empower, and serve people, motivating everyone around me to achieve my clearly articulated organizational focus of positively shaping the individual, organization, and society.
>
> ➤ Know what the strengths and motivations (Impact Niche) are for each Impact Player in my organization.
>
> ➤ Play to their strengths.
>
> ➤ Coach my Impact Players and let them play.
>
> ➤ Attempt to be a person of character, faith, and courage.

Step 2—Impact Leader Assessment

The strengths necessary to be an Impact Leader are somewhat different from the strengths of an Impact Player. It is necessary for an Impact Leader to accurately assess his or her own leadership strengths and weaknesses and play to the strengths. There are two ways to do this. One is to ask the Impact Players in your organization what they think your strengths and weaknesses are, and then add in your observations. The second is to take the Impact Leader Assessment. To take this assessment online go to www.ImpactPlayer.net.

Step 3—Team Assessment

To achieve Continuous Performance Improvement on a team-wide basis, an Impact Leader must accurately assess the strengths and weaknesses of each Impact Player on the team and play to their strengths. There are two ways to do this. One is to ask the Impact Players what they think their strengths and weaknesses are, and then add in your observations. The other is to have each Impact Player take the Impact Player Assessment.

Step 4—Set Goals

Outline the goals for your personal and organizational development. Be detailed and honest in your assessment on how you and your team are going to achieve them.

Step 5—Envision Success

Spend five minutes during the day with your eyes closed envisioning how well you are progressing as an Impact Leader.

Step 6—Congratulate Yourself

Every day, congratulate yourself first thing in the morning and right before you go to bed on being an Impact Leader. Review the transformation you are going through and the progress you have made.

* Note: For an example of The Impact Leader Assessment, please go to the APPENDIX section in the back of this book.

The Impact Player Awards: Recognizing a Diverse Team of Winners in the Game of Life

We live today in a globally interconnected world, in which biological, psychological, social, and environmental phenomena are all interdependent.
—Frtijof Capra, physicist

To be successful today, you must understand what the Impact Society is and what it requires. First, the Impact Society is an interdependent organism. The actions of the Big Six—not-for-profit organizations, business, academia, government, sports, and entertainment—cannot be separated. The Impact Society is a whole system. The decisions and actions of each one affect the others positively or negatively. Yet society today is divided into silos. This is not natural.

To break down these silos, the Impact Player Institute™ is proud to announce the Impact Player Awards.™

The Impact Player Awards

The Impact Player Awards honor people and organizations that excel at embracing change, diversity, innovation, and service to others while achieving unparalleled success in their field of expertise. The Impact Player Awards are the first awards that recognize individuals and organizations that are positively impacting the many stakeholders of society.

The Impact Player Awards will become the standard by which true success is measured. Some will argue that a select group of leaders should choose the winners. We believe the winners should be selected the same way the United States selects its leaders: by all the people. All members of society are invited to participate. Voting is held over the Internet.

It is the mission of the Impact Player Awards to focus an international spotlight on individuals and organizations that help all of society's stakeholders and are high achievers. When all of society sees the light, the world will become a better place in which to live. People can vote in a number of categories. Individuals

135

and organizations from business, government, academia, not-for-profit organizations, entertainment, and sports are all represented.

You can be part of the solution at www. ImpactPlayer.net.

Part 3

Innovation

For Everyone and Everything, the Only Thing Certain Is Change

It is not the strongest of species that survive, nor the most intelligent, but the one most responsive to change.

—Charles Darwin, evolutionist

You can replace the word "species" in the quote above with "individuals," "organizations," "companies," "governments," "cities," "regions," or "nations" and the statement will still hold true.

Innovation is a subset of Continuous Performance Improvement, and both are undeniably linked for corporations and geographical regions. Let's discover the secrets from some innovation experts.

Corporate Innovation

The genius of American capitalism since World War II is that we thrived on innovation that incorporated quality and value. There is always someone that can build it cheaper, but we built it better. Today, the United States has many innovative corporations. The most entrepreneurial ones, like General Electric and Johnson & Johnson, organize themselves like a bunch of little companies, with each division having their own operating infrastructure. From a distance this looks inefficient, but it works because it maximizes the entrepreneurial talents of its people.

—Dick Cavanagh, president and CEO, The Conference Board

A. G. Lafley

A. G. Lafley: Innovation and Change Leadership Go Hand-in-Hand

Few executives know as much about innovation as A. G. Lafley, chairman and CEO of Procter & Gamble. This is a guy who knocked down an executive cafeteria to make way for an employee-training center, who gave consumers a new spin on a product as common as a toothbrush. His insights are provocative but unquestionable:

"Change is inevitable, pervasive, and accelerating," Lafley says. "It's coming at us from more unexpected sources than ever before. Those who resist change will not survive. Those who adapt to change may survive, but they will not lead. Those who shape change, who turn it to their advantage and grow as a result of it, not in spite of it, win—often disproportionately.

"Leading change is the only way to play. It is the mindset that drives real innovation. However, change is hard. It's threatening. It involves risks that we can never be sure will pay out. It often has personal implications we don't want to deal with. It's human nature to fear change, but those who lead change harness that fear. They see change as an opportunity, not a threat.

"Change leaders do four things consistently well:

1. They are in touch with reality.

2. They anticipate alternate scenarios.

3. They make clear choices that produce advantage.

4. They inspire action in those around them.

"These are the skills that we cultivate in leaders at every level within Procter & Gamble. I'm firmly convinced that organizations that master change leadership are the most innovative, responsive, and ultimately successful organizations in any industry or field."

Procter & Gamble's Fine Fragrance business was facing a brutal situation in the mid-1990s. It had relatively low profits, was delivering low total shareholder return, and was losing much of its earnings in obsolete products. It was a "push" business—pushing the product to the customer.

Fragrances were designed based on the instincts of the company's "expert noses" voting on consumers' behalf. P&G's Fine Fragrances business changed the rules of the game by getting in touch with the consumer. They designed a new process— one that works so well that P&G is keeping it secret—that allowed consumers to talk to the company regularly about what fragrances made sense to them.

It's very difficult for consumers to really tell you about a fragrance, though. They know whether it's a light fragrance or a heavy fragrance, a sweet or fresh fragrance, but that wasn't much help. So P&G devised a sort of quiz for the nose, a set of questions that helps consumers paint pictures to compare their feelings about a scent to fabrics and colors. In the process, P&G developed a much more specific and insightful understanding of what customers wanted.

When P&G launched its Hugo men's fragrance, it went straight to Generation-X males, the key demographic. The company identified key people in trend-setting cities, such as London, New York, Paris, Rome, and Frankfurt, to engage young male consumers. It worked with them through every element of design. These prospective consumers had a say from the beginning in packaging, in-store materials, and advertising. Ultimately, P&G generated demand that transformed its Fine Fragrances business from a "push" to a "pull" model—rather than try to convince people they wanted the product, P&G had created a product consumers already wanted.

Hugo Boss is now the best-selling men's fragrance in the world. Even more impressively, it's the best-selling non-French male fragrance in France, the fragrance capital of the world. This is a terrific example of a business that stared reality in the face, got in touch with consumers, and demonstrated the decisive leadership needed to transform the business and emerge as a global winner.

Alan G. (A. G.) Lafley's Biography

Alan G. (A. G.) Lafley is chairman of the board, president, and chief executive of Procter & Gamble Company. He joined P&G in 1977 in marketing. He held a variety of positions across the company for twenty-three years. In 2000, he was elected president and chief executive. Since then, he has put P&G back on track to meeting its long-term goals by focusing on top brands, countries, and customers, superior consumer value, and improved cost and cash management. Further, he has set a clear vision for future growth. P&G's stock price has risen from $57 a share when he became chief executive to about $90. In 2002, he was elected chairman of the board.

A native of Keene, New Hampshire, he graduated from Hamilton College with a BA in History and from Harvard Business School with an MBA. Before joining P&G, he served in the U.S. Navy for five years. He is a director of General Electric, General Motors Corporation, and the Business Roundtable.

Joe Stimac

Joe Stimac and Innovation Vs. the Status Quo

People are very open-minded about new things as long as they're exactly like the old ones.

—Charles F. Kettering, inventor

The innovative idea usually flies in the face of conventional wisdom. More often than not, conventional wisdom has been the restraint for true innovation. Because "the vision" goes against the status quo, spokespersons for the status quo will be the loudest naysayers.

Time advances: facts accumulate; doubts arise. Faint glimpses of truth begin to appear, and shine more and more unto the perfect day. The highest intellects, like the tops of mountains, are the first to catch and to reflect the dawn. They are bright, while the level below is still in darkness. But soon the light, which at first illuminated only the loftiest eminences, descends on the plain and penetrates to the deepest valley. First come hints, then fragments of systems, then defective systems, then complete and harmonious systems. The sound opinion, held for a time by one bold speculator, becomes the opinion of a small minority, of a strong minority, of a majority of mankind. Thus, the great progress goes on.

—Thomas Babington Macaulay, historian

The Innovation Algorithm

"Innovation happens rapidly when the right question is asked," says Joe Stimac, CEO of AccuHire Corporation. He uses his proprietary innovation algorithm to solve complex and challenging problems quickly. "If you look closely at monumental leaps in innovation throughout history, you'll see one common thread: The right question was asked before any effort was expended in searching for the solution."

The wrong question has often resulted in years of product/service evolution. Wasted time and money could have been avoided if the right question had been asked in the first place. "Imagine the market leadership that a company could have had if it had the revolutionary product or service from the beginning," Stimac says.

Large organizations using his methodology include H&R Block, Time Warner Cable, Coca-Cola Enterprises, and Manpower Professional. He does consulting for Sprint, GTE, Lockheed Martin, DOD, StorageTek, and many other international organizations.

Stimac describes his methodology: "I have a whiteboard in my office, and I begin by writing a baseline question. I return throughout the day and improve the question. I again attempt to improve the question the following day and invite others to improve the question to the level, if answered, that would solve all of the challenges below it."

Stimac applied this very principle to the applicant management system he named AccuHire. "In hiring, the resume and keyword searches reigned supreme, so naturally my first question was how to extract key information from the resume faster. I came back the next day and improved the question to 'How can we extract key information from resumes faster and more consistently?'" Stimac invited staff and guests to improve the question. One guest wrote, "How can we speed up the entire application process and make better and faster selection decisions?" After a few weeks of struggling to improve the question, Stimac put a giant red X over the questions and wrote, "Are resumes even necessary?" The answer was a resounding NO!

"Once I realized that we were all focusing on the wrong component in the selection process, it was easy to create a truly innovative solution that would solve many of the problems posed by placing the emphasis on the resume, and do it quickly, efficiently, and much more systematically," he says.

"Recruiters need to have consistent information from each applicant in order to make an informed selection decision. Resumes do not contain the same information or present the information in the same order." This lack of structure forces the recruiter to read each resume and identify to what extent the applicant meets or exceeds the position's requirements.

Reading each resume is a time-consuming and inaccurate process, especially when compounded with the fact that most recruiters fill multiple positions and have limited knowledge of the success criteria of each position. The result is a highly subjective process that forces the recruiter to make assumptions about each applicant's abilities.

Stimac's questions resulted in the creation of a Position Builder that allows recruiters to quickly and easily build highly specific questions and answers that directly target the performance requirements of each job. Applicants are invited to:

1)   Apply online.

2)   Complete the online questionnaire (an improved checklist).

3)   Be instantly assessed and ranked according to how closely they meet or exceed the position's requirements.

A recruiter would know instantly which applicants met or exceeded the position requirements without having to read a single resume!

This simple innovation resulted in huge savings of time and improved accuracy in the initial stage of the selection process. Ask any recruiter how long it would take to process 500 resumes. Days? Weeks? With AccuHire, it takes less than one second. The result: better hires faster.

Instead of the checklist being manually completed after resumes arrive, it was standardized and moved in front of the resume. That was an immediate improvement in the selection process. "It wasn't a big change, but it made a huge difference to the companies who want to hire the best fast," Stimac says.

The second component of Stimac's questioning process involves creating a grid and identifying the key tasks and the key players who perform one or more of the tasks. By matching the task with the best solution/player, he and his clients gain two advantages in process improvement: speed and accuracy.

With the position-specific checklist online, the applicant and the computer do 95% of the work. Recruiters receive screened and ranked applicants and can take immediate action. There's no more guessing about whether an applicant has the right background, education, or work experience, or whether they would fit into a particular division.

Innovative and revolutionary, his idea was too much of a leap for some hard-line recruiters who still wanted to see a resume. "I fought the request at first but eventually gave in, and now invite the applicant to paste his or her resume at the end of the questionnaire," Stimac says.

What's the advantage to employers? Speed! Speed in knowing whom to give priority consideration, speed in hiring, and increased productivity are all benefits. By asking the right question initially, Stimac developed an innovative solution that gives leading employers the first draft pick every time.

Dr. James Canton

Dr. James Canton Equates Innovation with
Providing Greater Customer Value

Dr. James Canton has seen the future and warns to guard against complacency, not technology.
—The Wall Street Journal

Dr. James Canton is a futurist interested in clarifying the innovation landscape, a much-needed endeavor. He has counseled corporations and governments worldwide on innovation. Dr. Canton, known as the Digital Guru, is an adviser to the White House Office of Science and Technology and the National Science Foundation. He is on the advisory board of MIT Media Lab, Europe.

He says people don't understand what innovation is. He believes the confusion is like the fable of three blind men trying to describe an elephant when each touches only one part. Dr. Canton says innovation needs to be viewed holistically to be understood. For organizations to be successful, they must: 1) properly define innovation, 2) establish a standard of excellence for measurement, and 3) develop a process for implementation.

In business, the focus of innovation is on return on investment. One of Dr. Canton's clients is the Student Loan Finance Corporation, whose goal was to use innovation to create more value for customers and increase profits. The innovation was a new business strategy using technology. The result was doubled revenues.

In government, the focus of innovation may be on serving people better. Even in government, innovation must have clearly-defined goals. Leaders must understand where they are, where they want to go, and how they are going to get there.

Dr. Canton proposes to help combat the ignorance about innovation by making it a subject of study in high school and college. When a student graduates, he or she must be able to *Connect the Dots* around technology, business, and innovation. Unfortunately, too many of our institutions of higher education are silo-oriented. Studies like Chemistry, Physics, Computing, Global Economics, and Entrepreneurship are kept separate; when in reality they are interdependent. Innovation is about aggregation, not fragmentation.

Here's Dr. Canton's definition of innovation: "Innovation is that idea that pushes value to internal customers and external customers in the market." He says the definition of value requires a different matrix across various industries. Companies like Virgin, General Electric, IBM, and Microsoft "dance the new dance." General Electric, for example, saw the value of selling through the Internet and focused its innovation dollars there.

The overriding theme of Dr. Canton's organization, the Institute for Global Future, is that innovation must always be focused on providing value. Defining "value" is the first step to becoming truly innovative—and successful.

The most common mistake many people in business make is to assume that things exist or will continue to exist in a straight-line relation. This assumption is the death knell to a corporation, because it completely discounts the reality of constant change and the need for innovation.

> *There is no reason anyone would want a computer in their home.*
>
> **—Ken Olson, president, chairman and founder,**
> **Digital Equipment Corp., 1977**

Dick Lajoie

Dick Lajoie, CFO of Belcan Corporation: The Interrelationship of Leadership and Innovation

The innovation point is the pivotal moment when talented and motivated people seek the opportunity to act on their ideas and dreams.
— **W. Arthur Porter, engineering innovator**

"The innovation process begins with listening to what the customer has to say," Dick Lajoie declares. "It is the best way to both retain and enhance your company's potential. In today's increasingly competitive environment with rapidly evolving marketplaces, companies need to develop new ways to improve products and services.

"One approach is to form cross-functional teams with members from various departments who represent a useful mix of perspectives. For example, they could include finance, operations, sales/marketing, development, and engineering. The key is for everyone to be involved from project initiation to completion, not just in isolated stages. The focus is on the customer's perspective, not that of the company department or group.

"It has been my experience that these cross-functional teams work best if they employ a structured approach with a beginning-to-end methodology. This brings focus and an unbiased data gathering-and-analysis tool-set for decision-making. This process is broken down into five major components:

- Project scope—the boundaries that frame each individual initiative.
- Resource planning—the composition of the team's schedule.
- Data collection—the assembly of sample interviews, observations, questionnaires, etc.
- Data analysis—the methodology for gaining insight into customer perceptions.
- Course of action—the specific action items or steps that address customer concerns or take advantage of opportunities presented.

The Role of Leadership in Innovation

"Leadership is the key ingredient in the innovation process. It provides the focus that eliminates or greatly reduces the fragmentation and complexity that can result in being too slow to market, too confused to set objectives, or too timid to implement change.

"Leadership provides the three things that innovative and effective organizations always have:

- Vision—what you want to be in the future.
- Mission—what you need to do to create the future.
- Principle—what you choose to believe in as you work toward your vision."

The Role of Impact Players in Innovation

"Impact players can be thought of as those who bring promise to an organization. At Belcan, we think of a promise in the context of how we interact with our employees, our customers, our vendors, and the communities in which we work. We believe that a promise must be built on a firm foundation of attitude, belief, perseverance, honesty, and vision. The building blocks are many:

- The wisdom of preparation
- The value of confidence
- The worth of honesty
- The discipline of struggle
- The privilege of working
- The satisfaction of serving
- The power of suggestion
- The virtue of patience
- The rewards of cooperation
- The fruitfulness of perseverance
- And more

"Relationships build networks. 'Partner or perish' is the new buzz-phrase in business. Alliances are becoming the key to corporate-growth strategies. They are like a virtual company that allows you to compete more effectively against much larger businesses at lower cost while providing more complete customer service. Each alliance company now has more weapons in its arsenal to satisfy existing customers and realize opportunities with new ones.

"Relationships are formed by participation—in community as well as business activities. These activities require personal commitment—time, not money. In the final analysis, they lead to rewards in business development and, maybe even more importantly, in personal satisfaction.

"Optimizing your people starts with the CEO and his or her core strategy. Every company has to have a core strategy to be successful. Great CEOs teach this strategy to their employees, suppliers, and customers. This is what sets them apart from the competition. It's what they bring to the world of commerce.

"If your people know and understand the core strategy, they align their daily activities around it to ensure its success. Whether it's the CEO who sets the strategy, the engineer who then knows what to build, the salesman who then knows to whom to sell, the accountant who then knows how to price, or the clerical or production staff who then know how to administer or produce, each employee is caught up in moving the company in the same direction. Each feeds on the other to sustain the company's momentum and create the climate for overall success.

"Alliances will take center stage in the next five years. Knowledge maintenance and development is the key to increased productivity. Divide and conquer will again become watchwords, but in the new sense that teamwork is required to stay abreast of advancements in technology. Dedicated time and focus will be requirements for technological success. Everyone will be expected to take part in continuous learning activities. Decisions will become value-driven, not reactive or forestalled.

"It is my personal belief that greatness requires commitment. The quality of our work, the integrity of our people, and the willingness to listen to our customers are the cornerstones of success. If we respond to our customers' needs through creative solutions, if we encourage and support our employees in providing superior service, if we practice active leadership, we will enjoy success."

Dick Lajoie's Biography

Dick Lajoie is the chief financial officer, chief information officer, and president of ITD/MSD Belcan Corporation, an international provider of engineering, staffing, and information services. He served in the U.S. Army Infantry from 1969 to 1971 as a first lieutenant and was awarded various citations, including three Bronze Stars for actions in Vietnam. He received an MBA with major concentration in Accounting from Xavier University, Cincinnati, Ohio, in 1972 and a bachelor of Business Administration with a major concentration in Finance from the University of Notre Dame, Notre Dame, Indiana, in 1969.

Bob Messenger Discusses Innovation and the Consumer

He who rejects change is the architect of decay.
—Harold Wilson, former British prime minister

Since the consumer is such an important part of the economy, we wanted to *Connect the Dots* to see what the Impact Society's consumer would look like. We were fortunate to interview Bob Messenger, author of *The Morning Cup*, the food-and-beverage industry's number one daily news resource. Besides writing *The Morning Cup*, Bob is a consultant to top management in the food-and-beverage industry.

> *Your presentation at our management meeting was just what we needed. You made a lot of folks think about opportunities in fresh new ways.*
> **—Bruce Rohde, chairman and CEO,**
> **ConAgra Foods, to Bob Messenger**

Bob is an Impact Player. His insight allows businesses to *Connect the Dots* and discover where the consumer is driving the Impact Economy. He challenges executives to become visionaries and broaden their orientation. He gives them insights on where their industry is going. Bob's vision is applicable to all consumer-oriented industries. Here are some of Bob's thoughts, which all Impact Players should keep in mind.

Messenger's Message

"Visionaries have to look ten years out and give products and services to consumers now."
"Say something new about something old."
"Don't ask people for their time—they don't have any."
"Watch what people do, not what they say."
"Inspire people."
"Lifestyle changes will tell you everything you need to know about anything."

Bob believes corporate America has a significant hurdle to overcome. The "Universal Product" (soup, peanut butter, etc.) that could be sold to everyone in the world is dying because of private labeling and demographic changes. Consumers are demanding that companies tailor their products and services to meet the needs of different age groups or ethnic groups.

Consumers are spoiled, Bob says. They are demanding new tastes, new experiences, and convenience. (Don't ask me for my time. I don't have any.) In other words, consumers are demanding innovation to meet their lifestyle needs.

Those trends are irreversible, Bob says. Corporate America has to innovate or die. For that reason, vision is the most important quality an Impact Player can have. It is important to listen to customers in the innovation process, but sometimes Impact Players have to go beyond their customers' perspective. Impact Players have to analyze and synthesize information and invent something entirely new. Bob's favorite quote is something Henry Ford supposedly said: "If I had asked the people what they wanted, they would have told me faster horses."

Bob Messenger thinks winning companies in the food-and-beverage industry and other sectors of the economy will focus on these trends.

1) Convenience is the dominating force. People don't have time.

2) Packaging will be the main reason people buy. Does it convey ease of use and convenience?

3) The market for wellness foods will explode. Baby boomers will demand healthy food with medicinal ingredients.

4) The U.S. Hispanic market will demand the "Latinization" of products and services.

5) Food producers and restaurateurs from around the world will come to the United States to produce and serve products that are exciting to the U.S. Hispanic population. Some of these new competitors will be big winners.

Brand Innovation

Kleenex failed as a cold-cream remover. Repackaged as a disposable hand-kerchief, its success remains nothing to sneeze at.

—Unknown

Andrew Arken

Andrew Arken Says: "Tell a Story and Develop a Winning Brand"

Andrew Arken has more than thirty years of new-product-development experience at Procter & Gamble Company, where he led the test market and national launches of several successful brands. Let's read his thoughts on how innovation and storytelling go hand-in-hand.

"In this high-tech age, why should a business be interested in storytelling? People have been using stories to convey meaning and pass on values and life lessons for thousands of years, long before the development of written language. This discussion about stories is really about learning how to form *bonding relationships with customers or employees*. When you think about forming relationships, you have to appeal to someone on more than just an intellectual level; you have to connect on an emotional level. While objective data speak to the mind, stories speak directly to the heart."

The following explains how stories can have a direct impact on your customer and company bottom line.

1. **Stories can help you understand your consumer's unarticulated needs.**

Using storytelling as part of consumer interviews can help elicit the consumer's unarticulated needs. Examples include: 1) the Archetype approach, developed by Dr. Clotaire Rapaille, in which consumers are asked to write stories of their first and most impactive experiences with a topic (after going through a "guided imagery" exercise) and 2) the ZMET approach, developed by Dr. Jerry Zaltman, in which consumers use pictures they have chosen to reflect their thoughts and feelings about a topic as the basis for storytelling during a structured, in-depth interview.

2. **Having a story can lead to increased consumer awareness and trial for your brand.**

People are naturally *engaged* by a compelling story. Stories elicit a <u>multisensory, imaginative response</u>, with the listener bringing sights, sounds, smells, and multiple associations to the story. Your consumer can envision himself or herself interacting with your brand.

3. **Having a story can help create loyalty and empower brand advocates.**

Stories can impassion consumers. They elicit an *emotional response* such as love, humor, passion, etc. This can help drive *loyalty*, even leading to brand *advocacy*.

Advocates, in turn, can spread their own stories of positive interactions with your brand.

4. Having a story leads to team alignment with your brand identity.

A story's telling can become almost ritualistic, becoming the glue that can hold a team together and create consistency of action.

5. Having a story leads to increased team passion for your brand vision.

People are readily convinced by a compelling story. Stories inspire *commitment and intrinsic motivation.*

6. A story provides a source of continual creative replenishment to further build your business.

Stories are *enduring.* They have lasting value, but can evolve over time to keep the message fresh. Bringing a story to life unleashes the *creativity of possibilities* that moves beyond meeting basic product benefits and performance needs, into designing exceptional consumer experiences."

> *Via their brand story, Nike challenges consumers to transform themselves. It gives them a taste of the satisfaction that can be theirs if they "just do it," regardless of their age, gender, or abilities."*

> —Andrew Arken

There are several fundamental elements of a compelling story:

- ◆ **PREMISE.** The core or the heart of your expression. It is what you are communicating about human nature and the human condition.
- ◆ **CHARACTER DEVELOPMENT.** For the audience to personally relate to the story, the characters must grow or be transformed.
- ◆ **CONFLICT.** The core conflict of the story, its source of tension, is resolved in the climax. This is made particularly engaging via a hook, twist, or a surprise.
- ◆ **RICHNESS.** The development of subplots, side characters, or multiple levels of interpretation increases the potential for more universal appeal, more jumping-off places for creativity, and more points of alignment.

◆ **AUTHENTICITY**. Brand stories that are overtly false, or which mis-represent or exaggerate human needs or emotions will trigger negative reactions.

◆ **CATALYST**. In general, the customer should be the hero. The brand is the key catalyst. Over time, this catalytic brand positioning begins to define the character of the brand.

So how do you use a brand story?

1. Game-changing business strategy

By seeking opportunities to re-script your consumer's story, you unleash creativity that can redefine a category. Lenscrafters redefined the U.S. prescription-eyeglass market by "re-scripting" a vital but highly inconvenient need into a simple, pleasurable experience: "Quality eyeglasses in just one hour."

2. Holistic brand design

By taking the brand story's defining elements and translating them into design principles, the brand proposition can be more completely and consistently delivered to the consumer, making your brand proposition more personally relevant, provocative, emotional, and multisensorial to the consumer. Starbucks brings the Italian espresso bar experience to life. From the beverage names, product displays, ambience, and customer service, all elements are consistently delivering their brand story. A compelling story can lead to a strong brand *icon*. We know that consumers think in pictures, not words, and often communicate their pictures through stories. An icon can serve as a visual reminder of an entire story, such as the Energizer Bunny, who "keeps going and going…"

3. Team commitment and alignment

Making the brand story explicit in a credo or vision is a means of uniting teams toward a common passion and business objective. Ritz-Carlton's credo, "Ladies and Gentlemen serving Ladies and Gentlemen," is supported by real consumer-service stories that reflect respect and caring.

Action Steps

◆ Analyze stories obtained from customer testimonials or market research as well as project team members' stories about their current reality or their imagined ideal experiences. The team creates a shared story that is translated into a vision or credo.

♦　Translate the story elements into design principles through techniques such as language processing/KJ Analysis. Design principles drive brand execution (nomenclature, graphic/label/package design, consumer communication including copy, customer communication including display/shelf set, etc.).

From a corporate perspective, Disney can really be thought of as a "company of stories." The employees use stories of exceptional consumer experiences to re-energize themselves and to train new employees. When Disney Imagineers begin projects, they create stories that serve to identify design criteria and guide their work throughout a project.

—**Andrew Arken**

Q&A with Andrew Arken

Which companies do you think embrace innovation, and what makes them succeed?
In recent years, the company that really stands out to me as embracing innovation is Starbucks. They entered a declining coffee market and built a huge global business. In founder Howard Schultz's words, they "reinvented an age-old commodity." Instead of coffee being primarily a grocery or restaurant item, Starbucks showed it "could be a great experience, not just a great retail store." They didn't just offer a beverage, they offered customers "a taste of romance added to what otherwise might be an unremarkable day, an affordable luxury, a world-class reward anyone can afford, an oasis, a small escape during the day, a quiet moment to gather your thoughts and center yourself, and a casual social interaction, even if they didn't talk to anyone." All this started with a compelling vision by its leader, who conveyed his passion to those around him. *Creating and deploying a vision is a critical factor in innovation*, one that too many companies neglect.

What role does innovation play in wealth creation for a business?
I believe innovation has always been crucial to long-term business success, and in today's rapidly changing and highly competitive global market, innovation can even be critical in the short term. Continual-improvement type innovation keeps you competitive in the short term, but breakthroughs ultimately help you remain a long-term leader. The most innovative companies balance strong, established offerings with a continuing pipeline of new products and services. The really innovative companies make their own businesses obsolete rather than waiting for a competitor to do it.

Why is the customer experience so important in innovation?
I'm convinced that virtually all successful businesses are customer-focused. You might occasionally fool a consumer, but consumers are smart and will quickly target their spending where they perceive the greatest value to be. And to deliver that value, a company needs to have an in-depth understanding of its key customers' needs and then efficiently deliver its offerings in a quality way. This leaves lots of room for innovation in understanding customer needs and how those needs are delivered (encompassing production, service delivery, sales, and marketing innovation). Disney is a great example of a company that builds its business around thoroughly understanding its customers and delivering product and service experiences throughout the entire relationship, from awareness through repurchase, working to build long-term loyal relationships.

What makes innovation initiatives succeed or fail within organizations?
There is some good research on this subject showing a range of factors that are characteristic of innovative companies. In my experience, the following factors are critical to innovation:

a. Having and deploying a clear and compelling vision

b. Allowing employees more freedom to do their work

c. Encouraging risk-taking, reducing fear of failure

d. Having people work on projects they have a passion for and doing everything possible to stimulate rather than extinguish that passion; this is the basis for intrinsic motivation, which drives innovation

e. Focusing on nurturing ideas, not being overly critical

f. Finding a better balance between company and individual needs

g. Providing people with the tools/skills/resources/coaching they need

h. Getting management more involved in a supportive role, showing more trust

i. Removing excessive time constraints

j. Putting more effort toward building high-performance teams

k. Encouraging more fun in the workplace

l. Encouraging more hands-on work with consumers

m. Celebrating and using the diversity of our different styles

Is the pace of innovation going to increase or decrease in the coming society?
I expect the pace of innovation to increase. Globalization, better communications, new technologies, and better understanding of innovation and consumer needs will all increase competitiveness, requiring more innovation. My personal vision is that we will start treating personal creativity and innovation as critical elements of the education process, even for children, and that this will not only ultimately improve the bottom line for businesses, but will improve society as a whole as people become more intelligent about dealing with problems, managing change, and creating new opportunities.

Andrew Arken's Biography

Andrew Arken has more than thirty years of new product development experience at the Procter & Gamble Company, where he led the test market and national launches of several successful brands in the areas of fabric and home care, food and beverages, and health care, and contributed to the design and implementation of corporate marketing and market research models that have been deployed throughout the company. His innovation leadership also extended to the training and facilitation of individuals and business teams in new product development and creative problem-solving. He currently operates his own consulting company, specializing in innovation.

Regional Innovation

Regional innovation occurs in a specific geographic area. The premise is that for regional innovation to take hold, Impact Players from business, government, and academia must collectively develop and execute a plan. Continuous Performance Improvement among a cross section of Impact Players is a must for these regional innovations to succeed. Two of the premier Impact Players in the area of regional innovation and commercialization are Dr. Ralph Synderman and Dr. Bill Brundage. Dr. Brundage recently told the National Governors Association:

> Building the infrastructure for the knowledge-based economy is a team sport. It requires the collaboration of business, government, and academia and a blurring of the lines that separate their roles. Government will build and sustain a public policy that supports the three pillars upon which the New Economy is built: a thriving research-and-development capacity, an entrepreneurial business climate, and an educated workforce. Academia will supply the technologies. Business will convert the research into viable companies and provide the capital that those firms need to succeed.

Dr. Ralph Snyderman

Dr. Ralph Snyderman and Healthy Regional Innovation

With every business being swept along by the e-business revolution, there has never been a higher premium on the ability to innovate. I do not know how any company competes today without a thriving research and technical capability.

—Lou Gerstner, former CEO, IBM

The best way to do something right is to learn from the best. We interviewed Dr. Ralph Snyderman, president and CEO of the Duke University Health System, to see how Research Triangle Park became the regional innovation and commercialization powerhouse that it is today. The 7,000-acre Research Triangle Park is the largest research park in the United States, home to over 140 organizations. There are 42,000 full-time employees that come to work in the park each day.

"Research Triangle Park is a tremendous example of leaders from business, government, and academia working together to develop a region full of innovation and commercialization," Dr. Snyderman says. "State and local governments, along with the academic institutions of Duke, University of North Carolina, North Carolina State, and North Carolina Central, with the support of local businesses and international corporations like GlaxoSmithKline, have made the region a success."

Dr. Snyderman was quick to point out that Cambridge, Baltimore, Palo Alto, Ann Arbor, and Silicon Valley are other regions that excel at innovation and commercialization. However, he also noted that there are more hopeful regions than there is a market to support them.

He gives credit to the strong governorships of North Carolina in the late 1950s and early '60s for the vision that made RTP what it is today. Since moving to Duke from Genentech in 1989, Dr. Snyderman has enjoyed not only a strong working relationship but a friendship with North Carolina governors Jim Hunt and Mike Easley. To get things done and become an innovation and commercialization region, he says, governors must have an ability to move quickly.

Dr. Snyderman outlines what a region of innovation and commercialization requires:

1) An environment of community and trust among the Impact Leaders from academia, business, and government

2) A strong working relationship with large business partners, such as he has with GlaxoSmithKline

3) An area with strong research-oriented universities

4) A university faculty that appreciates the need to commercialize their innovations (At Duke, the learning curve began in 1989 and lasted into the mid-1990s.)

5) An infrastructure commercialization medium at a university (In Duke's case, Duke Translational Medicine, Inc.)

6) A strong grant-writing relationship with the National Institutes of Health and other federal research initiatives

7) A strong flow of solid ideas for venture capitalists from people with the talent to implement them

One other thing is required, Dr. Snyderman says: A network of Impact Leaders is critical to getting things done. The size of the network needed is in direct correlation with the size and scope of the initiative. For example, as Duke branched out overseas, his network of Impact Players began to include the best talent from Singapore.

Dr. Ralph Snyderman's Biography

Dr. Ralph Snyderman is chancellor for health affairs at Duke University Medical Center (DUMC) and president and CEO of the Duke University Health System. DUMC ranks among the nation's premier academic institutions. Its Health System offers a full continuum of care (from primary care to hospice) across a broad geographic area and is regarded as a national model for academic medicine. Dr. Snyderman is a nationally-renowned scientist (in the field of inflammation) and administrator. He is chair of the Council of Deans of the Association of American Medical Colleges.

Dr. William Brundage

Kentucky Innovation: A Strategic Plan for the New Economy by Dr. William Brundage

What would life be if we had no courage to attempt anything?
—Vincent van Gogh

Dr. Bill Brundage was recently appointed commissioner of the Office for the New Economy for the Commonwealth of Kentucky. Whereas Research Triangle Park is on the front line of innovation and commercialization, Kentucky is doing a great job at playing catch-up. Dr. Brundage was hired to help Kentucky become more competitive in the development and commercialization of technologies so desperately needed for the state to stay competitive with other regions. It's a must for business, government, and academia to work together in order to achieve regional innovation.

Strategic Plan

The Impact Players of Kentucky worked together and developed a strategic plan. Dr. Brundage, Governor Paul Patton, U.S. Senator Mitch McConnell, U.S. Congressman Hal Rogers, House Speaker Jody Richards, and Senate President David Williams spearheaded the development of *Kentucky Innovation: A Strategic Plan for the New Economy*. The plan was shaped by hundreds of people, serving on six regional-planning teams. These teams consisted of university administrators and faculty, businesspeople from large and small firms, the Kentucky Chamber of Commerce, teachers, local elected officials, legislators, and representatives of state agencies.

"The plan recognizes Kentucky's current position in the knowledge-based economy, identifies those New Economy niches where Kentucky might gain a competitive advantage within a decade, and establishes the public policy framework necessary to achieve results," Dr. Brundage says. "The plan acknowledges that business must lead the way to prosperity in the emerging economy while demonstrating how government can play an effective supporting role through public-private partnerships and by fostering an environment in which its New-Economy businesses, existing and new, can prosper. Moreover, the plan recognizes that Kentucky must continue to invest in a knowledge infrastructure, particularly at the postsecondary education level, to develop both the intellectual pool and the research-and-development capacity required for success in the emerging economy."

Intellectual Capital Development

Let's look at Kentucky's initiative for intellectual-capital development. Kentucky has a program called Bucks for Brains that finances endowed chairs and professorships at the University of Kentucky and the University of Louisville. This program combines public monies and private donations to attract and retain renowned researchers and faculty. These Impact Players are vital because they are responsible for future wealth creation. Wealth creation occurs through their innovations, which in turn are commercialized, producing revenue.

Bucks for Brains Highlights

Here are the highlights of the Bucks for Brains program at the University of Kentucky:

➢   The school has endowed 57 chairs and created 145 professorships.

➢   Already, 31 of those chairs and 86 of those professorships have been awarded.

➢   They have created 193 fellowships, scholarships, and endowments for research support and a library.

➢   They have hired 57 new faculty members, funded an average of 100 graduate research fellows and research assistants each year, and spent $5.76 million for new faculty startup expenses, lab renovations, and equipment.

➢   In fiscal 2002 alone, the faculty brought in $33 million in outside funding for sponsored research and projects.

To see much more to this broad and all-encompassing plan, visit www.one-ky.com.

Dr. Bill Brundage's Biography

Dr. William Brundage received his Ph.D. in Microbiology in 1967 from Louisiana State University after a tour of duty as a captain in the U.S. Army Medical Service Corps in Vietnam. He began his academic career as an assistant professor at LSU, followed by thirteen years at the University of Southern Mississippi, where he ultimately became the director of research and sponsored programs.

In 1982, he became president of the Southern Center for Research and Innovation, a not-for-profit organization that coordinated advanced-technology research with field applications in the local economy. He developed satellite technology for emer-

gency-medical-service systems that was used by government and media after the Mexico earthquake and the eruption of Mount St. Helens.

In 1987, he became the first president of the Kansas Technology Enterprise Corporation (KTEC), a quasi-public organization committed to creating and sustaining economic growth through innovation. Under his leadership, the KTEC became (and remains today) one of the premier technology economic development organizations in the nation.

From 1993 to 1997, he was president and chief executive officer of the Enterprise Florida Technology Development Board, a public/private partnership focused on creating high-wage jobs in technology-based businesses. In 1997, he founded his own consulting firm, American Innovation, Inc., and contracted with the Kansas City Area Development Council (KCADC) to establish the SmartTec Initiative. SmartTec is a technology economic development component of KCADC that was created for the purpose of increasing the number of high-growth-potential technology-based firms in the Kansas City metropolitan area. He then took on the role of interim executive director of the Kansas City Area Life Sciences Institute, a $300 million, ten-year bi-state community-investment program that fostered collaboration among two medical schools, four hospitals, and one major research center. Currently he is the commissioner for the Office for the New Economy in Kentucky.

Dr. Stuart Rosenfeld

Dr. Stuart Rosenfeld: Innovation via the Creative Enterprise Cluster

Society is joint action and cooperation in which each participant sees the other partner's success as a means for the attainment of his own.
—Ludwig von Mises, pioneering economic theorist

Impact Clusters™ are geographic regions occupied by Impact Players. Perhaps the foremost expert on workforce development and economic development in Impact Clusters is Dr. Stuart Rosenfeld, founder and principal in Regional Technology Strategies, Inc. (RTS).

RTS builds and accelerates regional competitive advantage by encouraging higher value-added commerce among highly-skilled people. A non-profit corporation called a 501(c)3 (for the relevant section of the tax code), RTS assists governments, foundations and other organizations in creating, implementing, and evaluating innovative regional economic-development strategies. In its work, RTS pays special attention to historically-disadvantaged regions and populations.

Because of cheap communication media, including the Internet, Impact Players can live anywhere. This has resulted in an important phenomenon that Dr.Rosenfeld is facilitating: the clustering of Impact Players. The new capitalism in the Impact Society is one of cooperation vs. competition within Impact Clusters. Successful clustering (originally called networking) is based on three principles:

1) Impact Players within Impact Clusters share resources they couldn't afford individually.

2) Impact Clusters focus on an Impact Niche that is design- and style-driven, not cost-driven. Why? Because cost-driven goods can be produced outside the United States, where people are paid much less. Dr. Rosenfeld calls these regions Creative Enterprise Clusters. Within these clusters are the artists, craftspeople, and others with specialized talents who focus on uniqueness and quality.

3) Impact Clusters that are industry-focused rely on a strong network of community colleges. Community colleges supply the mid-scale labor force critical to the growth of industry-based clusters.

The effectiveness of clustering is best illustrated in Maniago, which is in Friuli-Venezia Giulia, a region in Italy. This region features an Impact Cluster of artisans and companies that are experts in the design and manufacturing of knives.

Within this region alone, there are over 100 companies that focus on this Impact Niche. It is the sharing of intellectual capital between companies in the region that leads to their competitive advantage. In this instance, it is cooperation, not competition, that makes each Impact Player stronger in the marketplace.

Smart local, state, and national governments around the globe understand the clustering phenomenon and are using Dr. Rosenfeld's knowledge and research capabilities to help develop Impact Clusters within their geographic regions.

Here are some of the programs that Dr. Rosenfeld is involved with:

MetroVision Economic Development Partnership

RTS is performing a cluster analysis and developing a set of cluster "business plans" for the greater New Orleans region. At the same time, RTS is doing a commercial evaluation of intellectual-property portfolios and potential links to regional clusters and an assessment of technology-transfer practices and policies at research universities and medical centers in greater New Orleans.

Mississippi Clusters

RTS worked on strategic plans for three clusters in Mississippi: Communications Information Technology, Auto Manufacturers and Suppliers, and Forest Products and Furniture. It also developed a statewide plan for the state's community colleges with a cluster focus on workforce development.

Montana Industry Cluster Analysis

RTS is conducting a targeted analysis of existing and potential industry clusters for the State of Montana. RTS is identifying, on a regional basis, industry concentrations that have a competitive advantage in terms of workforce, location, and specialized services and supporting institutions. The study will determine regional competitive assets as well as gaps and inadequate linkages within clusters. The analysis is supported by the Montana Governor's Office of Economic Opportunity.

As The Impact Economy™ matures, three things need to happen in regions that produce durable goods:

1)   Manufacturing companies need to embrace change and innovation. They need to find a replacement product that focuses on design and style.

2)   New businesses need to focus on the power of clustering and intellectual capital.

3) Government and industry must support a strong network of community colleges.

Dr. Stuart Rosenfeld's Biography

Dr. Stuart Rosenfeld's interests include research and policy formulation for various states and regions on regional industry clusters and business networks, and particularly roles for technical colleges, all with an emphasis on less-populated areas. Dr. Rosenfeld has served on several committees for the National Academy of Sciences; testified before and reported to more than a dozen legislative, congressional, and Organization-for-Economic-Cooperation-and-Development committees; and published numerous papers and books on business networks, economic development, technology policy, and vocational education, including Competitive Manufacturing: New Strategies for Regional Development; Smart Firms in Small Towns; Significant Others: Exploring the Potential for Manufacturing Networks; Industrial-Strength Strategies: Regional Clusters and Public Policy; *and* Overachievers: Business Clusters That Work.

For five years, he has been principal investigator in studies and evaluations for the U.S. Departments of Agriculture and Education, the National Institute for Standards and Technology, the National Science Foundation, the Ford Foundation, the Alfred P. Sloan Foundation, and the Joyce Foundation, the German Marshall Fund of the United States, the North Carolina Rural Economic Development Center, the Appalachian Regional Commission, the Tennessee Valley Authority, and various states and regions. He founded and directs the activities of the Trans-Atlantic Technology and Training Alliance, an internationally-renowned network of leading technical colleges in the U.S. South and Europe.

Previously, Dr. Rosenfeld was deputy director of the Southern Growth Policies Board (SGPB), an interstate compact representing the governments of thirteen states and Puerto Rico, and founder and director of its subsidiary, Southern Technology Council. Before joining the SGPB, he worked for General Electric Company, where he managed an operations-research group and directed and helped design an advanced manufacturing-management education program. He later directed a private elementary school in Vermont. From 1977 to 1982, he was a senior associate at the National Institute of Education, where he designed and co-authored a national evaluation of vocational education, mandated by Congress. He holds an Ed.D. in Education Planning, social policy, and administration from Harvard University, an MS in Educational Philosophy from the University of Wisconsin-Milwaukee, and a BS cum laude in Chemical Engineering from the University of Wisconsin-Madison.

Regional Innovation and the Digital Divide

Hell, there are no rules here—we're trying to accomplish something.
                                                    —Thomas Edison

I visited over thirty cities in the United States to see which regions are implementing plans for innovation and commercialization and which ones aren't. Unfortunately, the Impact Economy will be a divided society. There are places like Ann Arbor, Baltimore, Kansas City, Salt Lake City, New York, Research Triangle Park, Denver, Austin, Reston, San Diego, Omaha, Dallas, Los Angeles, Lincoln, Louisville, Boston, and Chicago, where government, business, and academia are working together. They will prosper. But there are many regions that don't have this collaboration, and they are dying. They are suffering from "brain drain" because Impact Players go to areas that reward innovation and results and that promote diversity.

Entrepreneurial Innovation

Earvin "Magic" Johnson: The Impact of Urban Entrepreneurship

We see things not as they are, but as we are.

— Anais Nin, diarist

In late November 2002, I met Magic Johnson for the first time and heard him speak. Magic Johnson was back in Lexington, Kentucky, again. The University of Kentucky had tried hard to recruit Earvin Johnson for basketball after high school. Lexington was now recruiting him to help educate city leaders on how to revitalize urban economic development, and this time they got him. Listening to his speech, it was obvious that Magic's passion is for winning, no matter what the venue.

"The urban areas for years have been neglected and in decay," he said. "African-Americans and Latinos often times must travel tens of miles to shop at a grocery store or dine at a national restaurant chain, even though urban areas are heavily populated and people have money to spend."

That's the focus now of Magic Johnson, Los Angeles Lakers All-Star, League MVP, and world champion. He is the ultimate urban entrepreneur. Forbes Magazine estimates the annual sales of Johnson Development Corporation at $500 million.

Magic Johnson's recipe for success: leadership, innovation, and a partnering arrangement with Howard Schultz of Starbucks and other businesses with significant brand equity. His holdings include Magic Johnson Theatres, in partnership with Loews Entertainment, and Magic Johnson TGIF restaurants.

As a partner (not a franchisee) with Starbucks, he adjusted the menu to satisfy the wants of his clientele. Instead of cream puffs at his urban Starbucks, you'll find sweet potato pie. The background music is soft jazz.

To ensure community acceptance, he launches his neighborhood enterprises by working with leaders of the community, the Urban League, and area clergies. His advice to would-be urban entrepreneurs: "Partner with a person of color, innovate to meet your customers' needs, and work with community leaders."

Sounds like the magic in this Impact Player's success is common sense.

Dr. Jeffry Timmons

Jeffry Timmons: Innovation via Collision Entrepreneurship

*There will come a time when big opportunities will be presented to you,
and you've got to be in a position to take advantage of them.*
—Sam Walton, founder of Wal-Mart Inc.

Jeffry Timmons is a man whose name stands out in the minds of entrepreneurs, educators, students, and leaders when the term "entrepreneurial leadership" is mentioned. Over the last thirty-five years, he has led the charge in developing entrepreneurial education and research in the United States. When Michie P. Slaughter was president of the Ewing Marion Kauffman Foundation's Center for Entrepreneurial Leadership, she called him "the premier entrepreneurship educator in America." And why not? Jeffry Timmons has built Babson College into an Entrepreneurial-Studies powerhouse.

U.S. News & World Report, Success and *Business Week* have named Babson's entrepreneurial program first in the nation. Jeffry Timmons is the first person to hold a joint appointment at Babson and Harvard. Babson received a $30 million gift from the Franklin W. Olin Foundation in 1995, the largest ever gift ever received by a U.S. business school. Since 1995, Jeffrey Timmons has had an endowed chair in his name, recognizing his contributions to Babson and the field of entrepreneurship (endowed by The Price Institute and Babson faculty and friends). His focus now includes helping CEOs of emerging companies and developing leadership initiatives to help Native Americans seeking economic self-determination and community development.

I caught up with Professor Timmons on his way to New Zealand. His words were enthusiastic and optimistic. "The good news is, just because we are experiencing a downturn in the stock market and significant external threats doesn't mean creativity dries up," he said. "In spite of the phenomenon of bubble exuberance, society and the economy will move forward. Sure, we have experienced a pulling-back of the markets, but this is the reality of the capitalist system."

Professor Timmons identifies two of the important entrepreneurship trends today: 1) entrepreneurship is international in scope, and 2) "collision entrepreneurship" is part of the world economy.

"International entrepreneurship is being energized by the buddy system," he says. "More and more U.S. students and teachers are spending time overseas and vice versa. As a result, new ideas and relationships are being formed that foster stronger opportunities for new and emerging offerings. Over the last ten years, courses in both degree and non-degree entrepreneurial programs have been evident in Japan, China, Spain, Singapore, and Australia."

When the practical and the intellectual collide, that's collision entrepreneurship. Now relevant courses in entrepreneurship are taught by practicing entrepreneurs as well as Ph.D.s. Family companies can attend the four-day, four-night Price Babson Fellow Program. National accreditation has been changed so that 10% of the instructors can be non-Ph.D.s, opening the door to the likes of Bill Gates to teach classes.

The final aspect of collision entrepreneurship comes when students collide with the real world of business. There is a synthesis approach as educational silos are replaced with understanding and communication. The idea is for medical students, for example, to understand the framework of such things as entrepreneurship, finance, and the capital markets as well as medicine.

Professor Timmons emphasizes the positive: "Capital markets will find the true entrepreneur, and the entrepreneur will find the capital markets."

Demographic Shifts and Innovation

Knowledge itself is power.

—Francis Bacon

Demographics are shifting. A shortage of men and women in their prime working years is coming. The Hispanic population in the United States is exploding. The consumer is demanding more and better products and services. Generation gaps are splintering our organizations. The Impact Economy requires workers to have a new set of skills. Impact Players are demanding to be treated as partners, not employees. Impact Leaders need to be aware of what demographic shifts are occurring and what they mean to business.

Continuous Performance Improvement will only occur in nations, businesses, and individuals that are educated on demographic shifts.

Gary Wright

Gary Wright, Global Trends Expert

Knowledge exists to be imparted.
—Ralph Waldo Emerson, poet and philosopher

We interviewed Gary Wright, associate director of the Global Trends Group at Procter & Gamble, to give you an insight into his knowledge of changing demographics and what they mean for business.

"Demographics push industries around," Gary Wright says. The number-one demographics issue today is an aging population, the result of slowing population growth. Birthrates around the world are at unprecedented low levels (especially Spain, Italy, Germany, and Japan). The United States is the exception, with stable population growth. That stability plus immigration means the United States has the workforce to accomplish what needs to be done. Japan has resorted to trying to grow its population with incentives—what are called "pronatalist" policies. In the 1970s and 1980s, Sweden and East Germany tried incentives such as offering better housing, but with little success.

Around the world today, the old are getting older. In the United States, the baby boomers are getting older. The age of the "Golden Household"—a middle-income family with lots of children—is fading. Women are having fewer children. Women are waiting longer to have children. That means women have more time to themselves and more money to spend. The health-and-beauty market is growing because of that changing demographic.

The results of slower growth markets are intense competition, more mergers, and more business failures. As the Golden Household in the United States declines, the world will continue to change. The fall of the Berlin Wall, the fall of the Soviet Union, and the opening up of China really changed the scale of business. As the economies of those countries grow, more people will have more income to make purchases.

In the United States, the growth of the Hispanic population is a big demographic story. A high percentage of Hispanic households have children. The challenge for businesses in the United States is to make their traditional older executives understand the young Hispanic population. Businesses must recruit managers and employees that match the demographics of the consumer marketplace.

Gary Wright's job is to keep the company informed of changes that will affect its long-term success. He pushes information out to executives throughout Procter & Gamble. He increases his orientation by talking to a diverse assortment of people. His research shows that Americans still like to buy "things"—durables goods—rather than services. His research also shows that people actually have more leisure time, not less. They just feel they have less because of the time they spend watching TV or running errands for their children or grandchildren. Gary's final suggestion to business people is to watch what people are doing, not what they're saying. Actions don't lie.

Women in Business

Princeton University labor economist Alan Krueger, quoted by *Business Week Online*, says the return on investment in a college education is increasing more for women than for men.

Today, women hold more than 47% of executive, administrative, and managerial jobs, which is up from 34% in 1983. Women's share of professional specialties increased to 52% from 47% in the same period. There is no doubt those trends will continue. Why? It's simple: Women are motivated to be Impact Players.

Not only are women getting advanced degrees in record numbers, but they are on a mission to start their own businesses. The Center for Women's Business Research paints the picture:

> ➢ In 2002, there were 6.2 million privately-held women-owned firms in the United States.

> ➢ Women-owned firms employ 9.2 million people.

> ➢ They generate $1.15 trillion in sales.

> ➢ Women-owned businesses continue to grow at twice the rate of all U.S. firms.

> ➢ More than 1 in 18 adult women (5.7%) in the U.S. is a business owner.

Impact Mothers Have to Excel at Two Careers

Some of the real Impact Players in life today are the working moms that have to balance two careers: home and office. According to the working moms I interviewed, members of the household and their colleagues at work need and deserve the same things: support, recognition, face time, and a voice in matters. The three keys to running an Impact organization (both home and office), according to many working mothers, are to be organized, to be disciplined, and to treat people as individuals with the respect and dignity they deserve.

Many working mothers focus on compartmentalizing their two careers. Their families know that at work its work time and at home it's home time. One working mom I interviewed used the following schedule. She is home for dinner every day except one. On that long day she works until 2 a.m., in effect getting in an extra day of work. While at home she does office work only after the kids are in bed. As for weekends, that's family time. In order to nurture the "individual" within her children, each one has an established date night. On their date night they are able to choose the activity that most interests them. One of her daughters likes to go out to dinner, while another daughter prefers a quiet walk in the park.

The abilities to nurture the individual and serve the needs of others are attributes that seem to serve Impact Moms well in both careers. One Impact Mom I interviewed ran a division of a multimillion-dollar company. She had a colleague who was a single mom with a special-needs child. The child had a learning disability and professional testing was needed, but the mother didn't have the finances. The Impact Mom realized the right thing to do was to have the company pay for the testing—people need to know that people care about them. In this case, the company invested in the individual, which allowed the mother of the child to focus on her job instead of worrying about the child. The woman executive made the decision to help because it was the right thing to do. What the company received in return was a loyal worker who delivered unmatched productivity. The theme that this working mother goes by: "When you give to people they'll give back to you and more."

The largest network of working-women is an organization entitled the National Association for Women Executives (NAFE). As I learned in writing this book, networking is one of the keys to success and NAFE excels in this capacity. NAFE is the largest women's professional organization and largest women business owners' organization in the United States (125,000 members strong). When you need to excel at two careers, like working mother's do, make sure to surround yourself with a group of Impact Players that can relate and help you in your quest for success, peace of mind, and financial security.

Dr. Dotty Heady

Dr. Dotty Heady: A Leader in the Impact Society

It must be remembered that there is nothing more difficult to plan, more doubtful of success, nor more dangerous to management than the creation of a new system. For the initiator has the enmity of all who would profit by the preservation of the old institution and merely lukewarm defenders in those who gain by the new ones.

—Niccolo Machiavelli, sixteenth-century statesman

"There was not a lot to do in our small town, but we had a library, and I read everything I could get my hands on. When I was fourteen, I sat for several tests in math and science and earned a scholarship through the National Science Foundation in chemistry to attend Murray State College.

"I was young enough when I earned my first scholarship that I could still compete the next year in physics. I earned a scholarship in physics and later on was offered a full four-year scholarship in math at four colleges. I was told by one of the teachers that because I was a girl and good in math, I would make a good teacher. I said, 'Teacher! You don't understand, I want to be a scientist or doctor!' He shook his head, gave me a hard look, and said, 'No, *you* don't understand. You are a girl. Girls are teachers. Men become doctors and scientists. Besides, you'll probably get married and never finish school.' For him, that was the end of it. I wanted to prove him wrong. I couldn't understand why a woman could not be a scientist or doctor if she had the ability and that was what she wanted to be. There were other teachers, though, who not only encouraged me but inspired me in high school to go on to college.

"I began to see how women were treated differently in the business world. The dichotomy here is that I have become not only a doctor but also a teacher, and I have enjoyed teaching so much that I do not consider it work. It is fun to create an environment where people actually become curious and *learn* something; open their minds to think out of the box. I love it when I see the lights go on and a student really 'gets it.'

"In small ways, girls were pigeonholed or stereotyped into certain roles in society. My parents saved money for my brother to go to school and said I would marry and my husband would 'take care of me.' I laugh at this still, because it is so far from reality.

"One of the first times I applied for a job when I was still in high school, a man came out of his office and greeted me like this: 'Hi, honey, can you type?'

"I said, 'Well, yes…' and he put his arm around me and steered me to a group of women sitting at desks.

"He said, 'This is the typing pool. If you can type, this is where we'll put you.'

"I said, 'Thank you, but I can *think* as well as type and I *think* this is not the company for me after all.' I remember to this day the surprised look on his face and his open mouth as I left. He just didn't get it.

"I married the first time at seventeen, and my husband—and I cannot believe that I have to say this—would not let me take the four-year scholarship and finish college. He said he wanted a family and that I should work in the family business. This is what I did, and it didn't prepare me one bit for work when, five years later, I divorced him and became a minimum-wage worker with no college degree, trying to support two wonderful, busy small boys.

"So I began the process of working and putting myself through school while raising my boys. This meant that I worked two, three, and sometimes four jobs, seven days a week, to pay for my schooling to get to the point where I could feel like I had something to offer an employer and could expect to earn a decent salary.

"I modeled; sold shoes, diamonds, furniture and clothes; worked in a physician's office; kept books for five companies; partnered in a microbrewery; was a marketing director for a multi-location business; owned a day-care business; designed and performed executive training for business and industry; owned a food safety consulting business, traveling nationally and internationally; was executive director of a placement department for a multi-location business; taught live and on-line at the university level; received a gubernatorial appointment to the State Board of Proprietary Education; patented an invention; wrote manuals, grants, and a book for children; and served as chairman of the Board for Career Visions, an agency that helps the disabled find meaningful employment. Don't ever forget to give back.

"At one point, I was dubbed 'Queen of the Part-Time Jobs' and worked every vacation day for nine years straight. It is a good thing I have always had great energy, because even today, women have to work harder and still do not receive the same compensation that men do. It's better, but some companies still have a long way to go.

"You know I believe in education when I tell you that I earned associate degrees in Computer Science, Management, and Marketing; a bachelor of science in Marketing; master's degrees in Management and Marketing; and a doctorate of education in Leadership. I did all of this and working full time, teaching in the evenings to pay for my education, and I maintained a 4.0 GPA for all four years of my doctorate program.

"Impact Leadership is fascinating. Most people have some leadership skills, and leadership can *absolutely be taught*. It is a misunderstood topic and one of the most requested subjects for training in the country today. Sometimes when I explain the difference between a good manager and a good leader, people perk up. They identify with the concept and begin to talk about their strengths, their career paths, their passions about work, what they enjoy, and their dreams.

"The thing that I have discovered through business and teaching at the college level for the past ten years is that the things that happen to us as children can go on right into our adult lives. Many times, the students have told me that the hurtful or judgmental things that were said to them came from one of their parents, a family member, a good friend, a supervisor, or someone significant in their lives. It is difficult not to associate with those people when you are young.

"Someone asked me once, 'What made you think you could accomplish that?' and I said, 'What makes you think I couldn't?' I have had the highest numbers in the nation for two departments with two different companies. It is fun, and I like the challenge of doing the best in the country. Whatever the goal, it can be turned into a game, and I am determined to work any amount of hours to accomplish the goal and find a solution to the problem (opportunity). Once the problem is identified and the goals are met, I am ready to turn that situation over to a capable manager and move on to another challenge and develop the process to solve the problem again."

Dr. Heady epitomizes the definition of an Impact Player. Her focus is on results. She impacts everyone and everything around her in a positive way. Finally, her persistence to succeed no matter what the obstacles is dazzlingly evident. She continuously strives to better herself and to help those around her to succeed as well. Her story is evidence of how women will play such an important role in shaping the Impact Society.

The Impact Society and Diversity

Leaders interested in achieving Continuous Performance Improvement embrace diversity. All organisms seek to survive and prosper. For people in different age groups, "survive" and "prosper" mean different things. Older people who have wealth are looking to retain their wealth and work in an environment that is flexible to their needs. Younger people are looking to put their formal education to work and attain enough income to raise a family. In both groups, people want to be understood and respected. In the Impact Society, businesses must learn to adapt to the needs of their Impact Players. Impact Players will be of different ages and have different needs, which means compensation and benefit packages will vary from age group to age group.

One thing is certain: Change is the only constant. Age diversity and ethnic diversity are change agents for the Impact Society. Individuals, businesses, and organizations that segregate or isolate themselves and deny the demographic changes occurring in the United States and around the world dramatically increase the likelihood of their demise.

If an organization limits its membership to a homogenous group (color, age, sex), it might as well shipwreck itself on an isolated island with no food or fresh water.

Vibrant impact organizations display a full range of color and a wide variance in age. Diversity enhances the decision-making skills of an organization. Diversity maximizes the likelihood of survival.

The Impact Society is already showing the realities of the next fifty years. Global interdependence is the reality. Diversity is the norm. Impact Players are the influential part of this new world. People and nations that segregate and isolate themselves will suffer.

Eric Hoyt

Eric Hoyt: Diversity, Innovation, and the Global Economy Right Here in the United States

The wave of the future is not the conquest of the world by a single dogmatic creed but the liberation of the diverse energies of free nations and free men.
—John F. Kennedy

Eric Hoyt is CEO of Hoyt Americas. He grew up in Puerto Rico and has worked as a senior executive in Latin America and the United States for twenty years. Eric is bilingual and bicultural. He is an Impact Player who helps companies acquire and retain Hispanic and Latino customers in the United States.

Eric's experiences and subsequent Impact Niche are of benefit to all types of businesses, as his client list demonstrates. AOL Latin America, Club Med, and Hewlett-Packard are just a few of Hoyt Americas' clients. Eric believes the Hispanic business opportunity in the United States incorporates innovation but is also about solid, fundamental leadership skills based on listening, understanding, and acting. He is quick to say that the global economy exists right here in the United States. Businesses just need the knowledge and leadership to tap into this market correctly.

Eric grew up in what seemed to him the greatest place on earth: Puerto Rico. His military family moved from the U.S. mainland to Puerto Rico and never left. Why? Imagine a tropical island with white beaches and crystal-clear water, warm and loving people, an emerging industrial and economic awakening—and all part of the United States. Puerto Rico was, and still is, truly an exciting confluence of activities. But more importantly, Eric grew up bilingual and bicultural, a privilege that serves him well to this day.

Aside from reaping the obvious benefits of being able to speak two languages, he grew up in a marvelous mix of cultures that taught him understanding and respect.

Growing Up a Minority

Eric grew up an Anglo-American minority in the Latin culture. This experience helped him become an exceptional Impact Player.

He didn't know it at the time, but being a minority taught him to listen, to take nothing for granted, and to strive a little harder to be understood. The big win was realizing that it's quite all right that people think, act, and speak differently.

To Eric the key was listening, understanding, and adapting to get the most out of a presented opportunity. Those are not novel ideas, but ones at the heart of Impact Leadership: the ability to listen, understand, and act decisively.

The Numbers

There are more than 38 million Hispanics in The United States—one in eight people. That number has grown from about 4 million in 1950, or about 3%, to 13% today. And the growth will continue. The Census Bureau projects that by 2010, Hispanics will total 56 million: one of every five U.S. residents.

Hispanics still tend to be concentrated in California, Texas, Florida, New York, and Illinois, but increasingly they are spreading out across our country. Other top metro areas with Hispanic populations include Boston, Washington, Atlanta, Seattle, Salt Lake City, Colorado Springs, Detroit, Raleigh-Durham, Milwaukee, Wichita, and Minneapolis.

This Hispanic population puts the United States in the top five countries with Hispanic populations, led only by Mexico, Spain, Colombia, and Argentina. At our projected rate of growth, the United States will be the second-largest country of Hispanics by 2010.

Equally important, these Hispanic households have buying power. The mean household income for the U.S. Hispanic population by 2010 will be $45,701. Therefore, the market of Hispanics is big and growing and has money to spend. This is a market that merits a look by all companies. It could be argued that the global economy, or lack of it in some cases, is one of the key drivers fueling this growth of Hispanics in our country. In the same way companies expand distribution abroad in search of new markets, they can tap into this emerging market right here in our own country.

A Global Economy in the United States

The global economy exists right here! Instead of having to create new organizations or enter unknown foreign countries at significant cost, we can serve this market at home through existing business models. The companies most active in courting the Hispanic market are those that see this opportunity. By targeting the Hispanic segment, they are generating demand and new customers for their existing businesses.

Companies that focus on consumer packaged goods, financial service organizations, automotive companies, pharmaceutical companies, technology goods, telecommunication services, and media companies, Eric Hoyt points out, are all realizing the vast and profitable nature the Hispanic segment represents.

They need diapers and baby food.
They like white teeth, fresh breath, and clean homes.
They want to protect their money, save for retirement, and plan their children's education.

They want a home with nice furniture.
They want to live longer and healthier lives.
They like a cold beer with salty snacks.
They take pride in having a nice car.
They want to learn and improve their chances of success.
They enjoy television, radio, music, newspapers, and the Internet.
They love calling home and talking to family and friends.

I think you get Eric's point. Needs and values are global and cross-cultural. More and more of these companies are realizing that Hispanic consumers are very much like the classic mainstream American consumer. You just have to know how to speak to them and serve them. By listening, understanding, and acting, innovative companies are profiting handsomely.

Like mainstream marketing, marketing to Hispanics begins with solid consumer understanding. You quickly learn that the Hispanic community is diverse, and one size doesn't fit all. Mexicans dominate the Hispanic population in the West and Southwest. Cubans have traditionally been dominant in Florida, but this is shifting with an influx of Colombians, Venezuelans, Argentines, and Puerto Ricans. The Northeast and Midwest regions tend to see mostly Puerto Ricans and Dominicans.

Again, much as in the mainstream marketplace, companies marketing to Hispanics have different capabilities to address these cultural differences.

Respect

"Research consistently indicates that paramount to Hispanics are language, intent, and respect," Eric says.

The language aspect is pretty obvious, but it is not just a case of translating some ads or brochures or dropping a picture of Hispanic-looking people into your marketing materials. Done right, the answer lies in being genuinely committed to the segment. Consumers are not fools. This is where intent is key and, according to Eric, consumers can tell the difference between a Band-Aid solution and a real commitment.

From a marketing perspective, that means committing with front-end and back-end resources. Front-end resources are those investments geared to getting customers; back-end resources are those necessary to maintain and grow a relationship. The correct way means trying to attract new Hispanic customers while committing to an ongoing Hispanic community relationship. It's like the difference between a date and a marriage. A more complete and integrated approach to Hispanic marketing requires well-thought-out distribution, packaging, promotions, customer service, data understanding, and customer relationship management strategies.

A language strategy is nice, but focusing maximum business and marketing intent is smarter. Eric thinks every business has to ask, "What are we doing to get Hispanic customers, AND what are we doing to keep them, increase their number, and profit from them? Are you looking for a one-time transaction or a long-term profit stream?"

After twenty years in advertising and marketing, it still surprises Eric how obsessive companies are with acquiring new customers and how negligent they are with customer cultivation. The cost to acquire a customer is generally three to four times more expensive than to retain a customer. Long-term profitability lies in successfully managing and maintaining customer relationships.

Success Stories

For example, smart consumer-packaged-goods companies are profiting from acquisition and retention efforts. They go beyond targeted advertising in Spanish media to participating in community and grass-roots events. They create special packaging and customer service. They recruit and develop Hispanic talent within their company. The result is that their existing business models are enjoying expanded distribution, more customers, and a new marketplace with very positive outlook.

Eric once worked with a health-care services provider that came to him with a major churn problem among Hispanics. Superficially, it appeared that the Hispanic segment was highly disloyal and switched health plans frequently. After a closer analysis, Eric presented the client with a different explanation for the high churn rate: a disjointed marketing system that was based solely on acquisition with no emphasis on back-end performance.

Eric's solution centered on increasing the sales force's commission and changing the commission structure. In the existing model, commissions were based solely on applications approved; his team recommended increasing the salesperson's reward over time and under certain conditions—specifically, one-third payment upon approved application, one-third upon the member making the first visit to a physician, and one-third upon reaching a ninety-day membership milestone.

The key consumer insight was that once a Hispanic patient visits the physician and establishes the critical doctor-patient relationship, the likelihood of attrition drops dramatically. The recommendation regarding the sales force was even more obvious: pay them a little more and they will modify their tactics. The increased stream of customer payments and the reduction in processing costs easily offset the incremental cost of higher commissions. The fully-integrated marketing approach was less expensive and more effective.

Auto dealers are always challenged to "move the metal" off the lot. The zero-down, zero-interest, and zero-payment-for-ninety-days promotions are great for consumers but can wreak havoc on the manufacturer's and dealer's margin. The solution automakers are learning lies in understanding the lifetime value of the customer through ownership of vehicles over time.

The pressure to sell never goes away, but the importance of retaining and expanding the customer relationship remains paramount to the auto sales business model. Not only are ads and brochures targeting Hispanics specifically, but more and more salespeople and service personnel are bilingual, more financing programs are being developed and marketed in Spanish, and more call centers and customer-service functions are being modified to serve Hispanics, too. The result is not only more Hispanics going into dealerships to buy cars, but improved retention, profits, and brand loyalty among this segment.

Eric provides another example of customizing the business to the Hispanic market. A technology client asked his team during budget development how much they would have to increase advertising spending to support the next year's sales objective in Latin America. But Eric understood the client's business model well and knew that generating more demand was not the answer. The call center was already at full capacity. The problem was that the call-to-sale ratio in Latin America was about half what it was in the United States. Eric's team determined that every 1% improvement in call-to-sales conversion resulted in $1 million in revenue. The solution: better product training at the call-center for the Latin-American operators and selective use of incentives to those operators for improving conversion rates.

The results were predictable: The company's Latin-American operations reached U.S. conversion rates less than ninety days after the program was implemented, and sales skyrocketed—all without spending one extra dollar in demand-generation advertising! It was the right balance between front-end and back-end resources.

The Obvious Truth

The U.S. Hispanic market is growing and represents a great business opportunity, as Eric explained. A global economy exists right here in the United States. Leaders, innovators, and diversity advocates will benefit greatly from knowing this fact.

Developing an Innovation Culture

The human mind treats a new idea the way the body treats a strange protein: It rejects it.
—Peter Medawar, Nobel Prize-winning immunologist

Continuous Performance Improvement can only occur in an organization that has an innovative culture. Develop Innovation Impact Teams to change the corporate culture.

Many executives say they want an innovative culture but don't know how to go about changing the "company culture." Many Impact Players told us that what we have to do is find the innovation subculture and turn it into an innovation team. Providing the team with capital, a supportive environment, and a clear organizational focus is a necessity for success.

It's Like Politics

A little analogy from the political arena: A campaign manager doesn't spend a candidate's resources trying to get 100% of the vote. He targets the people who are likely to vote for that candidate. The idea is to motivate those people to persuade undecided voters. Once in office, the elected official shapes all of society. Getting a vote for the candidate is a simple return-on-investment model. Spend the money where you'll get the greatest return. The same holds true for innovation within an organization.

Develop a Network, Not a Bureaucracy

Innovation is stimulated by knowledge and information flows, a creative environment, and motivated people. The application of new ideas, knowledge, and innovations is where wealth is created.
—Nigel Oxbrow, founder and chief executive, TFPL Ltd, UK

Innovation Impact Team™ Ten-Step Program

To develop an innovative culture, an organization must develop an Innovation Impact Team supported by the highest-ranking executives. Here's how:

1) Develop an innovation team with the CEO intimately involved.

2) Spend the money on the existing innovation subculture and from this, assemble a team. Motivation won't be a problem.

3) If you want an innovative culture, commit the time and resources necessary for it to take hold. Commit to a well-thought-out initiative. Don't start and stop.

4) Membership on the innovation team should be as diverse as possible. For example, invite children to participate if you're a consumer-products company.

5) Take innovation team members away from the demands of their current jobs. It is virtually impossible to be innovative during demand time. The human brain doesn't function that way.

6) Provide the innovation team with business targets that impact the bottom line. The goals of solving a problem and creating revenue are great objectives. Give them clear organizational focus.

7) Position participation on the innovation team as the ultimate career objective.

8) Make the work of the innovation team very visible to all stakeholders.

9) Put experienced, talented, motivated professionals on the team. Include members of all age groups to help spread the word to the entire organization.

10) Send the members on the innovation team to events and workshops inside and outside the industry. Many great ideas have applications across different industries.

Innovation Team Example

The 5th International Chief Knowledge Officer's Summit was held at Luttrellstown Castle, Dublin, Ireland, on October 6–8, 2002. It was produced by TFPL Ltd, UK. Some of the participants included AIG, PricewaterhouseCoopers, British Telecommunications, AON, Burson-Marsteller, and others. A report from AIG substantiates the innovation team criteria:

"Within AIG, everyone has a charter to be innovative and to create new ideas and products. But people often hit a brick all trying to implement their innovation—lack of resources, availability of experts, and competition for time against the real job of making money! The solution was to create a new group of fifteen experienced people working in a rarefied environment away from the pressures of the business units. All were highly successful in the business and looking for change. The team was created for two years and was set the task of creating innovative new products and implementing them in conjunction with existing business units. They had revenue targets. After two years, the team had not only achieved its goals but was also now much more experienced and highly motivated, and its members moved into much better jobs within the business. The success of the project resulted in the next group attracting self-selected volunteers."

Idea Pirates™

> *The galleries are full of critics. They play no ball. They fight no fights. They make no mistakes, because they attempt nothing. Down in the arena are the doers. They make mistakes because they attempt many things. The person who makes no mistakes lacks boldness and the spirit of adventure. He is the one who never, never tries anything new. He is the brake on the wheel of progress. The very fact that he tries nothing, takes no chances, does nothing except criticize those who try, is perhaps the biggest possible error in a lifetime.*
>
> **—Anonymous**

Innovation is a hidden treasure that can be discovered only through exploration. Innovation lives in the minds of people. Innovative companies support exploration in an attempt to find this treasure. Unfortunately, many corporations don't explore, discover, and innovate because they are infected with Idea Pirates.

Pirates throughout history have plundered wealth and buried the treasure. Pirates are alive and well today, not on the high seas but in corporations and bureaucratic organizations. They are Idea Pirates. They use their power to suffocate innovation. They pillage people of their ideas, dreams, and innovations. Unfortunately, when pirates plunder, everyone suffers. Children are deprived of an exceptional educational experience. Cities lose their tax base. People lose their jobs as businesses go bankrupt. Leadership in an organization must allocate resources to the innovators in order to overpower the Idea Pirates.

Impact Players quickly recognize an organization wrought with Idea Pirates and will leave. If Impact Players are leaving an organization, it is probably infested with Idea Pirates. Executives must decide whether they want to lead an innovative company or captain a pirate ship.

Demand Time vs. Creative Time

Innovators understand the difference between demand time and creative time and the need for both. Demand time is the norm. Meetings are scheduled and held throughout the day. Creative time is time that is set apart to formulate new ideas and come up with new ways of doings things. It's virtually impossible to be creative during demand time. Ever wonder why some of your best ideas come while sleeping, fishing, or jogging? Innovation companies stress creative time as well as demand time.

Expanded Orientation

If the world should blow itself up, the last audible voice would be that of an expert saying it can't be done.

—Peter Ustinov, writer and actor

The companies that send their Impact Players to conferences, events, and workshops not only inside but also outside their industry are the ones that will promote and become innovative. It may be counterintuitive, but people who have mastered the core competencies of their work must be surrounded with Impact Players from other disciplines to become more valuable in their own industry.

The effective Impact Player analyzes and synthesizes information from an outside source into a new way of doing business.

Increasingly, the knowledge needed in a given industry comes out of some totally different technology with which, very often, the people in the industry are unfamiliar. No one in the telephone industry knew anything about fiberglass cables. They were developed by a glass company, Corning. Conversely, more than half the important inventions developed since the Second World War by the most productive of the great research labs, the Bell Laboratory, have been applied mainly outside the telephone industry. The Bell Lab's most significant invention of the past fifty years was the transistor, which created the modern electronics industry. But the telephone company saw so little use for this revolutionary new device that it practically gave it away to anybody who asked for it—which is what put Sony, and with it the Japanese, into the consumer-electronics business.

—Peter Drucker, management theorist

Kris Kimel & Joanne Lang

Innovation and the ideaFestival

Minds are like parachutes; they work best when open.
                    —Lord Thomas Dewar, epigramist

The Impact Economy is based on innovation and ideas. Kris Kimel and Joanne Lang are Impact Players who are focused on fostering the development of ideas through their international conference, the ideaFestival. (They're using the Sundance Film Festival as the model). The event is held in Lexington, Kentucky.

"The ideaFestival is a unique international event for the presentation, integration, and exploration of "big ideas" and innovation across a range of fields.

"All knowledge is part of a universal whole. The ideas and inspiration for new companies, products, designs, artistic endeavors, and more come from many different and often unusual places. Most people have little opportunity to be exposed to ideas and innovations outside their immediate field or area of experience. The ideaFestival provides a special place for the presentation, integration, and understanding of ideas and innovations across different domains.

"A crosscutting theme is selected for each festival. This focus provides an opportunity to explore in depth a particular big idea or innovation that has broad importance and implications. In addition to events directly related to the primary theme, each Festival has a broader array of idea activities (technology, art, film, etc.). The entire event is carried out over several days in a festival-type atmosphere involving a wide range of downtown spaces, activities, and locations.

"In 2002, nearly 7,500 people participated. Sponsors and attendees were intrigued by the unique focus of the festival and the opportunity to explore and discuss ideas that crossed a range of interests.

"We believe that quantum leaps in innovation will continue to occur as many of our long-held assumptions are proven false," Kris Kimel says. "We also believe that serendipity plays a big role in innovation. If we can get some of the greatest minds together asking 'What if?' who knows what innovations will occur." The next ideaFestival is scheduled for the fall of 2004.

2002 ideaFestival Impact Players who made presentations:

Richard Florida is the author of the groundbreaking book, The Rise of the Creative Class: And How It's Transforming Work, Leisure, Community, and Everyday Life *published in 2002 by Basic Books. He is the H. John Heinz III Professor of Economic Development at Carnegie Mellon University. Florida earned his bachelor's degree from Rutgers College and his Ph.D. from Columbia University.*

Brian Greene *is the author of* The Elegant Universe: Superstrings, Hidden Dimensions, and the Quest for the Ultimate Theory. *He is a Columbia University professor of Physics and Mathematics and graduate of Harvard University and Oxford University, where he was a Rhodes Scholar.*

Richard Gott *is a professor of Astrophysics at Princeton University and is noted for his contributions to cosmology and general relativity, which are discussed in his fascinating book* Time Travel in Einstein's Universe. *Gott earned a degree in Physics from Harvard, received his Ph.D. in Astrophysics from Princeton and was a postdoctoral fellow at the California Institute of Technology and Cambridge University in England.*

Margaret Wheatley *writes, teaches, and speaks about radically new practices and ideas for organizing entities in chaotic times. She is president of The Berkana Institute, a charitable global foundation serving life-affirming leaders around the world.*

Part 4

Aggregation

Aggregation

Are you looking to continually improve your performance in all aspects of your life? If you answered yes then this section is for you. Webster defines aggregation as "a group, body, or mass composed of many distinct parts or individuals."

Webster defines fellowship as "a community of interest, activity, feeling, or experience." Fellowship, according to Webster, is also "the state of being in the company of equals or friends."

If you combine the definitions of aggregation and fellowship you come up with my definition of "team." A team is composed of many distinct parts yet it is the state of being in the company of equals. Although we are all different, we are all the same. When the members of the team all believe in Continuous Performance Improvement, you then have a winning team. As Governor Martha Layne Collins, Dick Traum and Dr. Kevin Elko stated earlier, you need to be part of a team to truly perform at your highest level. Therefore, individuals that believe in Continuous Performance Improvement must be part of a team.

Here's where I need the help of Impact Players from around the country. Why not create a formalized league of teams based on the aggregation and fellowship of Impact Players? Imagine what it would be like if the league focused on helping its members to continually improve their performance, at work and in the community. If you would like to be part of this vision, you can be.

Announcing the formation of the
Impact Player League (IPL).

In the IPL, Impact Players from business, government, sports, education, non-profit, and entertainment gather together in localized teams. Each team works to promote education, inspiration, innovation, and fellowship. Teams then compete against and learn from each other. The focus is on becoming better leaders and helping each other reach their full potential both personally and professionally. The long-term result will be a legacy of which our children can be proud.

The Impact Player League:
A Challenge for Society

We're All in the Game of Life Together

Belief

While writing *Connect the Dots…To Become an Impact Player*, it became apparent to me that people, businesses, and cities achieve success based on whom they know, what they know, and by serving others. I believe all of society would benefit from a truly racially- and socially-integrated organization of Impact Players that focused on building relationships among leaders based on healthy competition and shared experiences. To meet this end, we have formed The Impact Player League (IPL). We believe it provides an invigorating and entertaining environment in which leaders from all walks of life will excel.

Chapter Cities

The Impact Player League will consist of franchises in cities across the United States (and eventually in cities around the world). Each city has a team name, i.e., the New York Vision, the Atlanta Insight and the Louisville Trailblazers.

Network of Networks

As membership grows the IPL will become the network of networks for Impact Players. Continuous Performance Improvement is the mantra. For example, members of the Louisville Trailblazers will be invited to meet with the members of the New York Vision. As Louisville meets New York, new friendships will be made, new business opportunities will arise, and the knowledge of every individual in attendance will grow as life's experiences are shared among members. The aggregation of minds is a beautiful thing, resulting in Continuous Performance Improvement at the highest level.

The Impact Player League: Be Part of a Team

People reach higher levels of performance when they are part of a team. Why wouldn't you join a team of Impact Players?

The Impact Player League builds cultural and fellowship bridges, resulting in wealth creation, knowledge transfer, and a clearer perspective of the real world for our members. These bridges allow members to discover the knowledge of different people, synthesize it, and create new knowledge. This new knowledge allows people to be innovative and create a better product or service, which results in wealth creation. When an Impact Player from one walk of life partners with a person from another walk of life, innovation and wealth creation will occur naturally. The fellowship of IPL members is a special bi-product that will be ingrained in society forever.

The IPL wants members who aspire to be part of a team and want to be something more than they are by themselves. The Impact Player League is creating a movement where everybody wins. The IPL is offering its members an opportunity to create wealth for their companies, organizations, and themselves by partnering with Impact Players of varying backgrounds.

IPL doesn't want people who are satisfied with the way things are. We want people who embrace diversity, change, and innovation. We want people who challenge the status quo for the betterment of all. Finally, we want people who appreciate and value the power of the human spirit.

The Impact Player League empowers people to look through a new pair of eyes. The Impact Player League and its diversity model enables us to see the changes that are taking place in the marketplace and society. This new vision allows individuals, businesses, and cities to take advantage of these changes before the competition does. The advantage results in better decisions and better leaders.

The Impact Player League helps members reach their potential by broadening who they know and what they know through chapter meetings, Impact Player roundtables, workshops, Impact Player conferences, The Impact Player Certification Program and The Impact Player Challenge.

The goal of The Impact Player League is to place a team in every major city throughout the United States and then expand globally. Team members of one team will meet other team members in person, on the phone, and via the Internet.

The Coach

As you know, every team needs a coach. Continuous Performance Improvement and coaching are like peanut butter and jelly—they go together naturally. Let's read what people are saying about one of the executive coaches of the Impact Player League, Dr. Kevin Elko.

Kevin Elko has shown both me and my team how to motivate ourselves and achieve emotional balance so we don't become too high or too low, but stay focused on the current game situation.

—**Emmitt Smith**
All-Pro running back, Dallas Cowboys and Arizona Cardinals

Kevin has the unique ability to touch everyone he speaks with. Nobody walks away from listening to Kevin speak without picking up something that makes them a better person. If I had one choice for someone to work with my firm, I would pick Kevin. He has the unique ability to touch people, to help people become the kind of person that they want to be.

—**Andy Kalbaugh,** president and chief executive officer,
American General Securities, Inc.

There is no doubt in my mind that one of the major reasons we were able to turn the program around at the University of Miami was Kevin Elko. He taught the players valuable lessons about focusing, performance anxiety, and how to handle adversity as well as success. He was instrumental in teaching the coaches to adapt their teaching skills to each individual athlete on a one-to-one basis. Kevin had a major impact on the entire program and will be equally as valuable in years to come, as we rebuild the Cleveland Browns.

—**Butch Davis,** head coach, Cleveland Browns

When Dr. Elko addressed us, we loved him. I found myself repeating his stories for days. He is inspiring and just what we needed.

—**Margaret Baldwin,** CFM, vice president,
senior financial consultant, Merrill Lynch

The Competition

Winning and losing are a part of life. Teams will compete against one another. Points are scored for the addition of new members on the team, the diversity of the team, the number of partnerships that came about due to being part of the team, the number of new services or products developed, the incorporating of the physically and mentally challenged into your workforce, the number of times that people of different races socialize, the amount of community service work, the number of people who go through Impact Player certification, etc.

Each team will have an Impact Player Captain (IPC). Impact Player Captains are former collegiate or professional Impact Players in athletics who are community leaders. The reason for having IPCs is that their positive appeal will attract youth and all members of the community. Impact Player Captains are excellent public speakers and are active members of the Impact Players Speaker's Bureau, which focuses on spreading the value of leadership, innovation, and diversity.

We look forward to expanding the Impact Player League around the world! But we need Impact Players. If you are interested in starting or joining a franchise of the IPL, please visit **www.ImpactPlayer.net** for more information.

Purpose

The Impact Player League exists to:

1) Empower individuals to reach their full potential, both personally and professionally, through Continuous Performance Improvement exercises.

2) Create wealth for individuals, businesses, and cities by fostering business partnerships and social relationships between people of all races.

3) Facilitate the production and distribution of relationships, knowledge, and ideas, resulting in innovation and wealth creation.

4) Develop the leadership skills of all people in an organization, not just a selected few.

5) Introduce leaders to other leaders from different segments of society so the very fabric of society is made stronger because of diversity.

The minds of people and the connectivity of these minds are where ideas are generated and where wealth is created. Just look at MIT, Silicon Valley, and Research Triangle Park. Technology is a tool, but human capital is the fuel for value creation. The asset of human capital is optimized through relationships and interactions.

The key question, then, is: Why wouldn't Impact Players want to join the Impact Player League? After all, the IPL is the medium for relationship building, knowledge accumulation, idea generation, and wealth creation.

Personal and professional optimization is created by innovation, and innovation occurs from the free flow of ideas in a diverse group.

The Impact Player League Excels in the Impact Economy.

In the physical economy, wealth creation occurs through discovery of a physical asset, like oil, and its subsequent ownership. In the Impact Economy, which is the direction the economy is moving, wealth creation occurs through discovery of a knowledge asset, an idea, and then ownership—a patent or new product or service.

In the physical economy, the people and businesses that help companies locate and mine a physical asset, such as oil, provide an extremely valuable service. In the Impact Economy, the people and businesses that help professionals, businesses, and cities locate and develop ideas are extremely valuable.

In the physical economy, companies that help change a physical asset, such as oil, into a more valuable commodity, such as gasoline, create value and are rewarded with wealth. In the Impact Economy, companies that facilitate the development of relationships and the transfer of knowledge into ideas that result in new and better ways of doings things (value creation) are extremely important to wealth creation.

The Impact Player League was designed specifically for the Impact Economy. IPL helps individuals, businesses and cities compete and thrive in the knowledge world.

The Aggregation of Impact Players

As the lines between business, academia, non-profit organizations, sports, entertainment, and government blur, it is obvious that leaders from all of these areas need to communicate with each other for personal, economic, and regional development. The Impact Player League actively recruits Impact Players from business, sports, entertainment, government, and academia for membership. Diverse input is one of the keys to current survival and future growth.

It is evident that for individuals, businesses, and cities to be successful today and in the future, they must develop a diverse network of leaders both locally and internationally. The focus of all leaders must be not only to meet a diverse group of people locally but also to develop social relationships and business partnerships with national and international leaders. They must establish a fellowship. They more time spend in fellowship, the more each one will have invested in one another and the more they care about one another.

Non-restrictive Membership

Unlike other organizations, the Impact Player League does not restrict membership to CEOs or presidents only. The Impact Player League believes that the decentralization of power within organizations and the growth of entrepreneurship require that leadership be taught to everyone in an organization. Furthermore, many of the world's greatest leaders are in roles that focus on serving others; we want these Impact Players to be part of the IPL. In the Impact Society, mission-critical decisions are made throughout the organization, not just at corporate headquarters.

Blind Spots

If you don't surround yourself with people of knowledge from diverse disciplines and backgrounds, then you have personal and organizational blind spots. And just like blind spots in cars, blind spots in one's orientation are dangerous. You don't have an accurate picture of what's going on in the marketplace, and that leads to poor executive decisions, some of which can even be fatal for organizations.

In Summation

Impact Players practice Continuous Performance Improvement. If you want to be the best, you have to surround yourself with the best. It's that simple. You may rationalize that you don't have the time or the money, but those are just excuses. The Impact Player League awaits those who strive to be the best that they can be. If you're ready to reach your full potential, please visit us at **www.ImpactPlayer.net**.

Afterword

Your Legacy Starts Today

No one's death comes to pass without making some impression, and those close to the deceased inherit part of the liberated soul and become richer in their humaneness.

—Hermann Broch, novelist

It became evident to me while writing *Connect the Dots...To Become an Impact Player* that personal success cannot be separated into compartments of one's life—business, personal, and social. The successful people I interviewed talked about all-encompassing success. Their message is that success engulfs the entire person and organization. Of course, that doesn't mean successful people or organizations are perfect. Quite the contrary.

Successful people are calculated-risk-takers. On their journey, people make poor decisions in business and in life because they take risks. The key is that successful people and successful organizations learn from their mistakes and move forward. Any successful entrepreneur has probably failed at one business or another. Look at how many career changes most of us make before we find the perfect job.

Striving to be successful is so important because of our legacy. The word legacy is usually associated with presidents and royalty, but whether we realize it or not, all of us will leave a legacy to our children, grandchildren, neighbors, friends, co-workers, and the world.

Legacy is defined by Webster as "something transmitted by or received from an ancestor or predecessor." Sure, successful business people leave their heirs money, but the real value they leave behind is how they lived their life. Why? Because the people close to you will use your legacy to model their own lives. The more parts of your life that people emulate, the more successful your life will have been.

His heritage to his children wasn't words or possessions, but an unspoken treasure, the treasure of his example as a man and a father.

—Will Rogers, Jr.

221

I chose the Thoreau quote "We were born to succeed, not to fail" to open *Connect the Dots...To Become an Impact Player* because if you take away one thing from this book, it should be that thought. All of us have something special to offer the world. *We are all Priceless Originals.*

Predictions for the Impact Society

Security is mostly a superstition. It does not exist in nature, nor do the children of men as a whole experience it. Avoiding danger is no safer in the long run than outright exposure. Life is either a daring adventure or nothing.
            —Helen Keller, advocate for the disabled

Thank you for taking time out of your hectic day to read this book. If you are striving to be an Impact Player then this book was written for you.

Let's close with some observations and predictions:

➢ An Innovation degree will become the most valuable major in education.

➢ The key to a person's value in the marketplace is whether he or she is an Impact Player.

➢ People who focus on improving their Impact Niche—what they can do better than others—will have job security.

➢ Demographic shifts in age and ethnic composition will dramatically affect business and government in the United States and the world.

➢ Businesses that understand and cater to the U.S. Hispanic population will prosper.

➢ Generational bridge-builders will evolve to solve misunderstandings between generations in the workplace.

➢ In the United States, new political parties will emerge as age, education, and race differences cause large traditional groups to become disenfranchised with the Republican and Democratic parties.

➢ Knowledge is and will continue to be capital.

➢ "Analysis-and-Synthesis Professional" will be a new high-paying occupation.

➢ The sheer volume of information will force corporations to move from a "push" to "pull" information-delivery system.

➢ Entrepreneurship will be taught from kindergarten through eighth grade.

➢ Interactive media will replace textbooks.

➢ Universities will act as holding companies and become major revenue generators.

➢ Most Impact Players will be independent contractors and entrepreneurs and work in Impact Clusters.

➢ Impact Players will demand lifelong education and development training from their employers.

➢ Consumers will demand more convenience.

➢ Wellness products and services will be in high demand as baby boomers age.

➢ Globalization and Latinization will come to the United States; companies from around the world will come to the United States and develop specialized products and services for the huge Hispanic market.

➢ Spending on talent assessment, training, and performance improvement will rise dramatically.

➢ Innovation will lead to new industries not even thought of yet.

➢ Leadership Networks of Impact Players that partner and share knowledge and relationships with each other will explode in importance.

➢ Impact Leaders will run organizations. Their most important job will be the successful execution of a well-thought-out vision that balances the needs of society, Impact Players, and shareholders.

➢ Organizations that can recruit and retain the best Impact Players will prosper.

➢ The number of women in leadership roles will increase dramatically.

➢ The most successful businesses will manage information and knowledge, but lead people.

➢ Three types of innovation will continue to grow in importance: regional, corporate, and entrepreneurial.

➢ Innovation Teams will reside in every successful organization.

➢ Innovation will be the key to new wealth creation.

➢ Idea Factories will be developed.

➢ Many new innovations in business will come from children.

➢ Innovation will be both evolutionary and revolutionary.

➤ Cities where business, government, and academia work together will thrive.

➤ Innovation will be used to solve problems as well as create new products.

➤ An innovation algorithm that focuses on asking the right question will change the world as we know it.

➤ Individuals, organizations, and regions resistant to change and innovation will die.

➤ Chief Innovation Officer will be a new executive position, reporting directly to the CEO.

➤ Traditional companies that use innovation to say something new about an old product will prosper.

Appendix

Impact Player Assessment Example

Success _Can_ Be Predicted ®

August 25, 2003

<table>
<tr><td colspan="2">Personal & Confidential</td></tr>
<tr><td>Name:</td><td>ROBERT MILLER</td></tr>
<tr><td colspan="2">Impact Player Assessment</td></tr>
</table>

SAMPLE REPORT
Go to www.ImpactPlayer.net to take this assessment.

Skill scores over 50% for any specific profile component indicate a likelihood of successful performance of that skill. These skill measures were developed on large samples of working people and 50% indicates average. This is very different from school grades where below 70% is failing. If a skill score is less than 50%, you exhibit this factor to a lesser degree. No one person exhibits all skills and behaviors at levels that exceed 50%. We are individuals each possessing a unique mix of skills at various levels.

If you score well on a specific skill measure, it means that your approach to exercising those skills is similar to those who do well. Any individual is likely to need exposure to effective tactics and an opportunity to practice before demonstrating your full potential in a given skill. Likewise, people may have high skill potential in many areas and choose to focus on a few out of preference for one career opportunity over another.

The validity scales from the Self-Descriptive Index indicate that you were candid in completing the questionnaires. As a result, the following interpretation is an accurate description of skill potential.

Summary of _Impact Player_ Skills

According to Chally's analysis of your assessment, the following Skills are most critical to success as an _Impact Player_:

Impact Player Skills	Score
SKILL FOR THE JOB	50%
MOTIVATED TO EXCEL	57%
HIGH ENERGY TO EXECUTE	62%
SELF-DISCIPLINE TO WORK LONG HOURS	77%
PERSISTENCE	92%
BURNING PASSION FOR RESULTS	49%
POSITIVELY IMPACT OTHERS	77%
COMMITMENT TO SERVE CUSTOMERS	57%

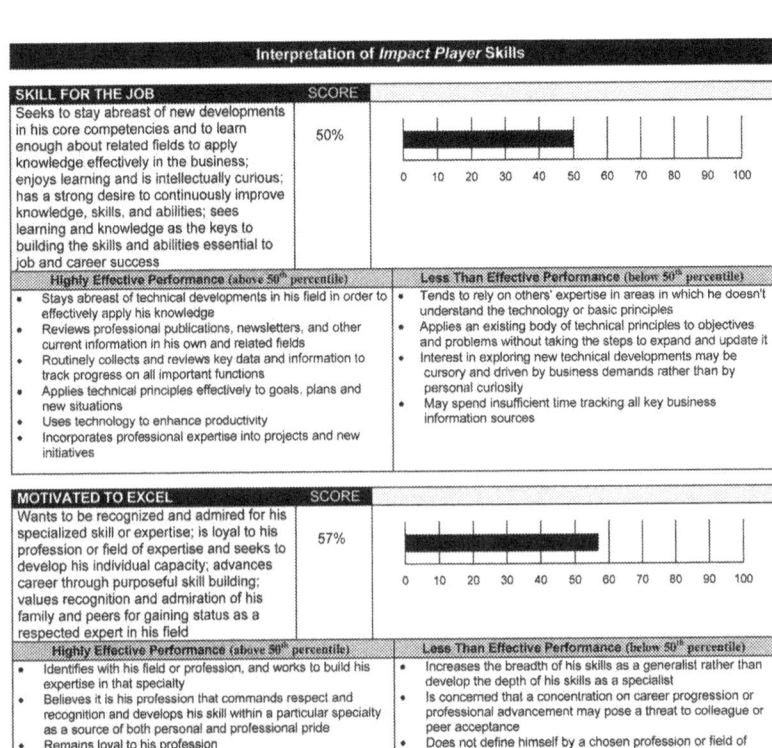

Interpretation of *Impact Player* Skills

SKILL FOR THE JOB — SCORE 50%

Seeks to stay abreast of new developments in his core competencies and to learn enough about related fields to apply knowledge effectively in the business; enjoys learning and is intellectually curious; has a strong desire to continuously improve knowledge, skills, and abilities; sees learning and knowledge as the keys to building the skills and abilities essential to job and career success

Highly Effective Performance (above 50th percentile)
- Stays abreast of technical developments in his field in order to effectively apply his knowledge
- Reviews professional publications, newsletters, and other current information in his own and related fields
- Routinely collects and reviews key data and information to track progress on all important functions
- Applies technical principles effectively to goals, plans and new situations
- Uses technology to enhance productivity
- Incorporates professional expertise into projects and new initiatives

Less Than Effective Performance (below 50th percentile)
- Tends to rely on others' expertise in areas in which he doesn't understand the technology or basic principles
- Applies an existing body of technical principles to objectives and problems without taking the steps to expand and update it
- Interest in exploring new technical developments may be cursory and driven by business demands rather than by personal curiosity
- May spend insufficient time tracking all key business information sources

MOTIVATED TO EXCEL — SCORE 57%

Wants to be recognized and admired for his specialized skill or expertise; is loyal to his profession or field of expertise and seeks to develop his individual capacity; advances career through purposeful skill building; values recognition and admiration of his family and peers for gaining status as a respected expert in his field

Highly Effective Performance (above 50th percentile)
- Identifies with his field or profession, and works to build his expertise in that specialty
- Believes it is his profession that commands respect and recognition and develops his skill within a particular specialty as a source of both personal and professional pride
- Remains loyal to his profession
- Advances his career by becoming more expert in his field
- Works to earn the title and credentials that demonstrate successful progression in his career

Less Than Effective Performance (below 50th percentile)
- Increases the breadth of his skills as a generalist rather than develop the depth of his skills as a specialist
- Is concerned that a concentration on career progression or professional advancement may pose a threat to colleague or peer acceptance
- Does not define himself by a chosen profession or field of expertise and is not likely to emphasize professional status as a career goal and source of personal satisfaction

HIGH ENERGY TO EXECUTE — SCORE 62%

Keeps up a brisk pace without becoming fatigued; pushes physical resources to the limit during periods of peak demand; prides himself on the amount of work accomplished; approaches work with considerable energy and stamina despite distractions or unreasonable demands

Highly Effective Performance (above 50th percentile)
- Maintains a demanding pace
- Prides self on being a hard worker and getting a lot of work accomplished
- Demonstrates a high degree of stamina or endurance and enjoys keeping active
- Typically produces a much higher output than average

Less Than Effective Performance (below 50th percentile)
- Can become fatigued if work demands get too high and needs a break to recharge
- Does not feel a need to accomplish a high volume of work
- Activity level does not remain consistently high and may tend to push beyond comfortable physical limits

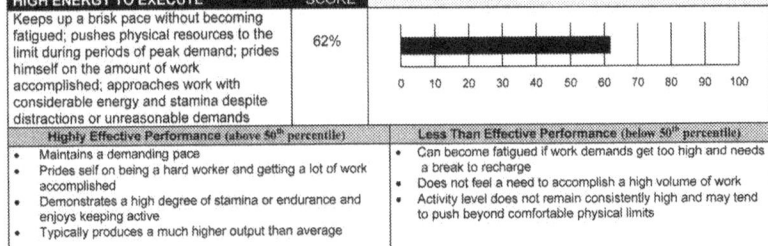

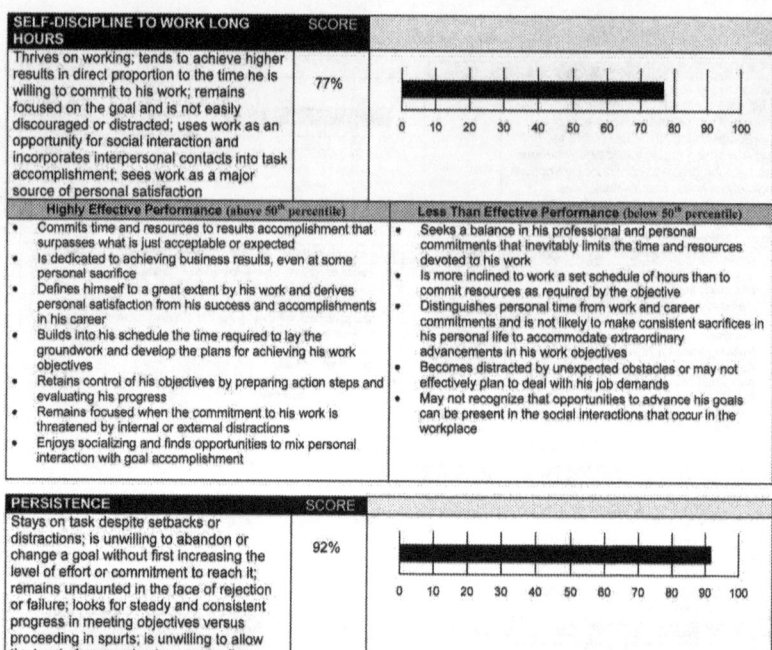

SELF-DISCIPLINE TO WORK LONG HOURS	SCORE	
Thrives on working; tends to achieve higher results in direct proportion to the time he is willing to commit to his work; remains focused on the goal and is not easily discouraged or distracted; uses work as an opportunity for social interaction and incorporates interpersonal contacts into task accomplishment; sees work as a major source of personal satisfaction	77%	

Highly Effective Performance (above 50th percentile)	Less Than Effective Performance (below 50th percentile)
• Commits time and resources to results accomplishment that surpasses what is just acceptable or expected • Is dedicated to achieving business results, even at some personal sacrifice • Defines himself to a great extent by his work and derives personal satisfaction from his success and accomplishments in his career • Builds into his schedule the time required to lay the groundwork and develop the plans for achieving his work objectives • Retains control of his objectives by preparing action steps and evaluating his progress • Remains focused when the commitment to his work is threatened by internal or external distractions • Enjoys socializing and finds opportunities to mix personal interaction with goal accomplishment	• Seeks a balance in his professional and personal commitments that inevitably limits the time and resources devoted to his work • Is more inclined to work a set schedule of hours than to commit resources as required by the objective • Distinguishes personal time from work and career commitments and is not likely to make consistent sacrifices in his personal life to accommodate extraordinary advancements in his work objectives • Becomes distracted by unexpected obstacles or may not effectively plan to deal with his job demands • May not recognize that opportunities to advance his goals can be present in the social interactions that occur in the workplace

PERSISTENCE	SCORE	
Stays on task despite setbacks or distractions; is unwilling to abandon or change a goal without first increasing the level of effort or commitment to reach it; remains undaunted in the face of rejection or failure; looks for steady and consistent progress in meeting objectives versus proceeding in spurts; is unwilling to allow the level of personal enjoyment to dictate his/her level of commitment to a task or directive	92%	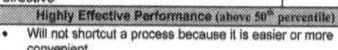

Highly Effective Performance (above 50th percentile)	Less Than Effective Performance (below 50th percentile)
• Will not shortcut a process because it is easier or more convenient • Tenacious and committed to staying on task • Will persist through even repeated failure • Recognizes repetition and hard work as critical ingredients to success • Will stay on point despite distractions by outside influences	• Believes that success is the result of luck or circumstance rather than persistence and focus • Could be deterred by rejection or failure • Could be distracted from his original focus • May not persist through seemingly insurmountable odds • Willing to take the risks associated with cutting corners or taking shortcuts • Looks for the hot ideas that will lead to quick success

BURNING PASSION FOR RESULTS	SCORE	
Able to sort through bureaucracy, complexity or politics to focus on required results; is not caught unprepared when obstacles are encountered; meets self-imposed standards of excellence by delivering agreed upon results	49%	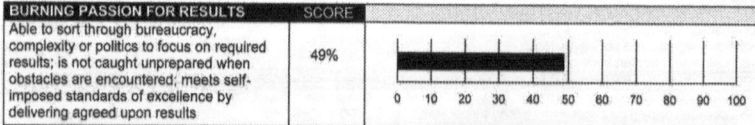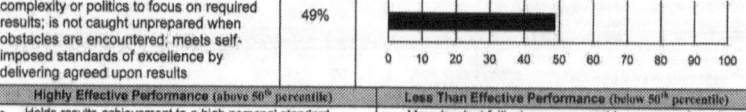

Highly Effective Performance (above 50th percentile)	Less Than Effective Performance (below 50th percentile)
• Holds results achievement to a high personal standard • Sets the criteria for ensuring successful results in accordance with defined requirements • Delivers the result that was promised without unnecessary fanfare or embellishments • Realistically anticipates barriers to results accomplishment and is prepared to respond • Cuts through administrative or political red tape to maximize his results accomplishment	• May view 'not failing' as an acceptable measure of results achievement • Uses his own criteria to determine goal requirements • May focus more on style and making a good impression than on content and relevance in results achievement • Assuming 'no news is good news', can be caught off-guard by unexpected obstacles • May revise his commitments when faced with unanticipated barriers rather than be on the lookout for problems and prepare to resolve them as they arise

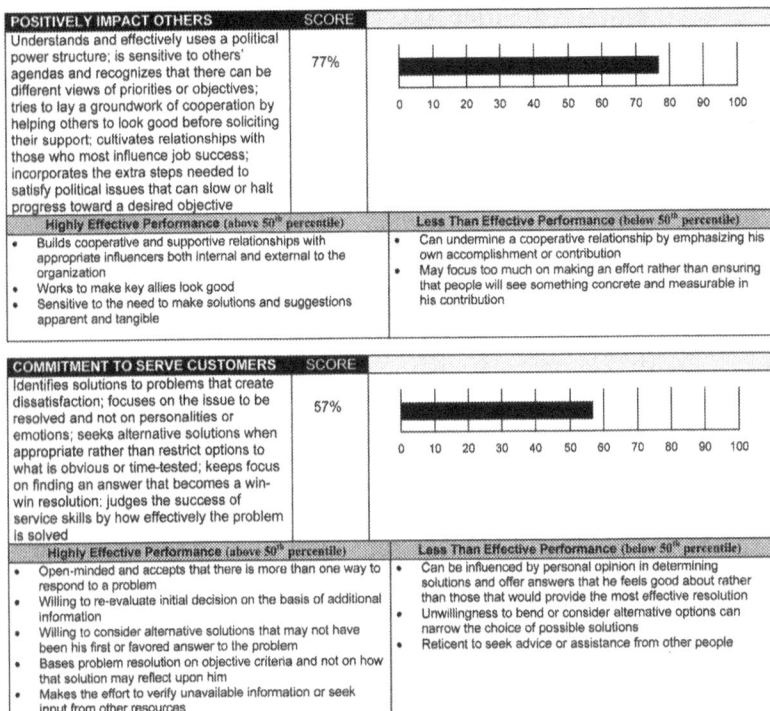

POSITIVELY IMPACT OTHERS	SCORE
Understands and effectively uses a political power structure; is sensitive to others' agendas and recognizes that there can be different views of priorities or objectives; tries to lay a groundwork of cooperation by helping others to look good before soliciting their support; cultivates relationships with those who most influence job success; incorporates the extra steps needed to satisfy political issues that can slow or halt progress toward a desired objective	77%

Highly Effective Performance (above 50th percentile)	Less Than Effective Performance (below 50th percentile)
• Builds cooperative and supportive relationships with appropriate influencers both internal and external to the organization • Works to make key allies look good • Sensitive to the need to make solutions and suggestions apparent and tangible	• Can undermine a cooperative relationship by emphasizing his own accomplishment or contribution • May focus too much on making an effort rather than ensuring that people will see something concrete and measurable in his contribution

COMMITMENT TO SERVE CUSTOMERS	SCORE
Identifies solutions to problems that create dissatisfaction; focuses on the issue to be resolved and not on personalities or emotions; seeks alternative solutions when appropriate rather than restrict options to what is obvious or time-tested; keeps focus on finding an answer that becomes a win-win resolution; judges the success of service skills by how effectively the problem is solved	57%

Highly Effective Performance (above 50th percentile)	Less Than Effective Performance (below 50th percentile)
• Open-minded and accepts that there is more than one way to respond to a problem • Willing to re-evaluate initial decision on the basis of additional information • Willing to consider alternative solutions that may not have been his first or favored answer to the problem • Bases problem resolution on objective criteria and not on how that solution may reflect upon him • Makes the effort to verify unavailable information or seek input from other resources	• Can be influenced by personal opinion in determining solutions and offer answers that he feels good about rather than those that would provide the most effective resolution • Unwillingness to bend or consider alternative options can narrow the choice of possible solutions • Reticent to seek advice or assistance from other people

THE ASSESSMENT DATABASE

The assessment you recently completed has been intensively developed, validated, and standardized on large samples of successfully employed management, technical, sales, administrative, and other skilled individuals. The database includes over 400,000 individuals.

ASSESSMENT RELIABILITY

The assessment measures motivation and relevant skills you have acquired over time. The results for most people are highly reliable and stable over time. This means that for people who take the assessment, over 90% will have nearly the same results from one year to the next. This does not imply that people cannot change . . .only that most people do not. If, at the age of 20, you like baseball and don't like horror movies, the chances are that at age 60, you'll still like baseball and avoid horror movies. Note, also, that for most people, short-term circumstances usually do not affect the results, i.e., having a good or bad day will usually not change the scores.

ASSESSMENT ACCURACY

While no assessment can be perfect, our standards for accuracy are quite high. In general, 95% of the people who review their own results feel that the assessment was 95% accurate in describing them. Often, if some part of the results does not seem to fit, it is a good idea to ask a close friend or family member to also review the results. If they agree with the results, it is likely that this is an area you are less conscious of and represents a blind spot in your own self-awareness.

We hope this information has been useful. These questionnaires were developed carefully and represent a modern, scientific method of assessment. The reliability of these results will fade with time since individuals can change. Data more than one year old should be re-evaluated.

Impact Leader Assessment Example

Success *Can* Be Predicted ®

August 25, 2003

SAMPLE REPORT
Go to www.ImpactPlayer.net to take this assessment.

Impact Leader Assessment

Skill scores over 50% for any specific profile component indicate a likelihood of successful performance of that skill. These skill measures were developed on large samples of working people and 50% indicates average. This is very different from school grades where below 70% is failing. If a skill score is less than 50%, you exhibit this factor to a lesser degree. No one person exhibits all skills and behaviors at levels that exceed 50%. We are individuals each possessing a unique mix of skills at various levels.

If you score well on a specific skill measure, it means that your approach to exercising those skills is similar to those who do well. Any individual is likely to need exposure to effective tactics and an opportunity to practice before demonstrating your full potential in a given skill. Likewise, people may have high skill potential in many areas and choose to focus on a few out of preference for one career opportunity over another.

The validity scales from the Self-Descriptive Index indicate that you were candid in completing the questionnaires. As a result, the following interpretation is an accurate description of skill potential.

Summary of *Impact Leader* Skills

According to Chally's analysis of your assessment, the following Skills are most critical to success as an *Impact Leader:*

Impact Leader Skills	Score
REALITY VISIONARY & COMMUNICATOR	50%
INNOVATOR & CHANGE AGENT	57%
APPRECIATES DIVERSITY	62%
INSPIRATIONAL LEADER	77%
RESULTS ORIENTED COACH	92%
SERVE OTHERS	49%

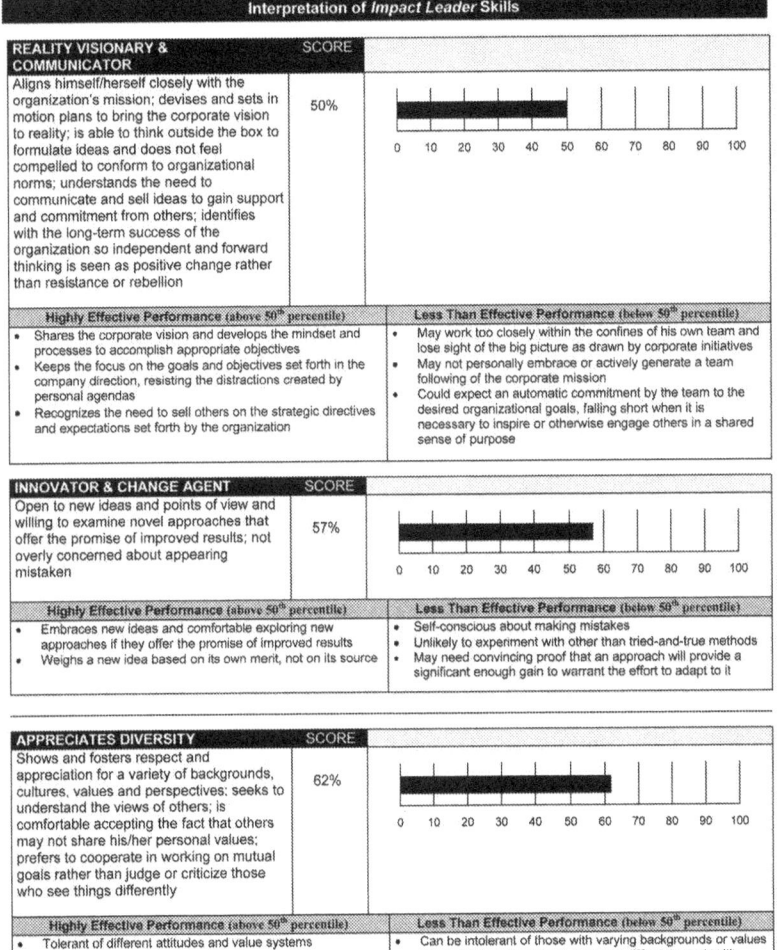

Interpretation of *Impact Leader* Skills

REALITY VISIONARY & COMMUNICATOR — SCORE 50%

Aligns himself/herself closely with the organization's mission; devises and sets in motion plans to bring the corporate vision to reality; is able to think outside the box to formulate ideas and does not feel compelled to conform to organizational norms; understands the need to communicate and sell ideas to gain support and commitment from others; identifies with the long-term success of the organization so independent and forward thinking is seen as positive change rather than resistance or rebellion

Highly Effective Performance (above 50th percentile)	Less Than Effective Performance (below 50th percentile)
• Shares the corporate vision and develops the mindset and processes to accomplish appropriate objectives • Keeps the focus on the goals and objectives set forth in the company direction, resisting the distractions created by personal agendas • Recognizes the need to sell others on the strategic directives and expectations set forth by the organization	• May work too closely within the confines of his own team and lose sight of the big picture as drawn by corporate initiatives • May not personally embrace or actively generate a team following of the corporate mission • Could expect an automatic commitment by the team to the desired organizational goals, falling short when it is necessary to inspire or otherwise engage others in a shared sense of purpose

INNOVATOR & CHANGE AGENT — SCORE 57%

Open to new ideas and points of view and willing to examine novel approaches that offer the promise of improved results; not overly concerned about appearing mistaken

Highly Effective Performance (above 50th percentile)	Less Than Effective Performance (below 50th percentile)
• Embraces new ideas and comfortable exploring new approaches if they offer the promise of improved results • Weighs a new idea based on its own merit, not on its source	• Self-conscious about making mistakes • Unlikely to experiment with other than tried-and-true methods • May need convincing proof that an approach will provide a significant enough gain to warrant the effort to adapt to it

APPRECIATES DIVERSITY — SCORE 62%

Shows and fosters respect and appreciation for a variety of backgrounds, cultures, values and perspectives; seeks to understand the views of others; is comfortable accepting the fact that others may not share his/her personal values; prefers to cooperate in working on mutual goals rather than judge or criticize those who see things differently

Highly Effective Performance (above 50th percentile)	Less Than Effective Performance (below 50th percentile)
• Tolerant of different attitudes and value systems • Accepts different viewpoints without personal bias	• Can be intolerant of those with varying backgrounds or values • Can judge individuals who are more difficult to work with

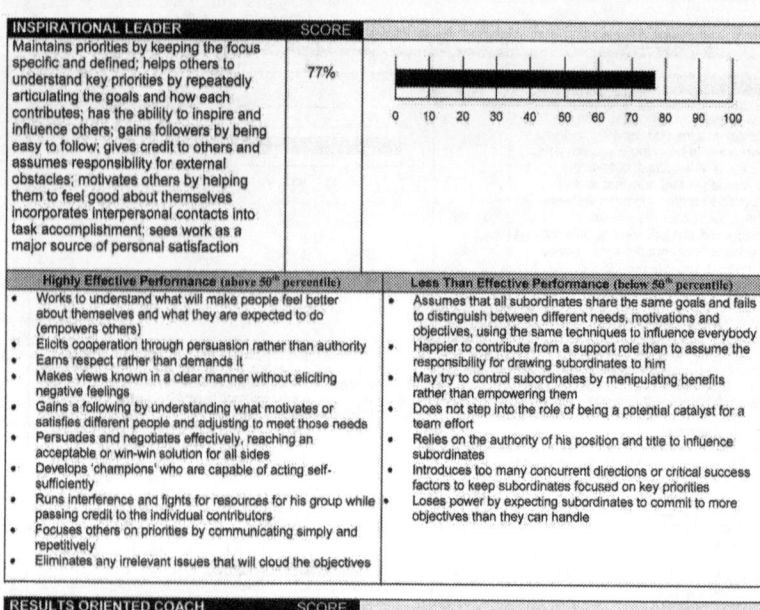

INSPIRATIONAL LEADER	SCORE	
Maintains priorities by keeping the focus specific and defined; helps others to understand key priorities by repeatedly articulating the goals and how each contributes; has the ability to inspire and influence others; gains followers by being easy to follow; gives credit to others and assumes responsibility for external obstacles; motivates others by helping them to feel good about themselves incorporates interpersonal contacts into task accomplishment; sees work as a major source of personal satisfaction	77%	

Highly Effective Performance (above 50th percentile)	Less Than Effective Performance (below 50th percentile)
• Works to understand what will make people feel better about themselves and what they are expected to do (empowers others) • Elicits cooperation through persuasion rather than authority • Earns respect rather than demands it • Makes views known in a clear manner without eliciting negative feelings • Gains a following by understanding what motivates or satisfies different people and adjusting to meet those needs • Persuades and negotiates effectively, reaching an acceptable or win-win solution for all sides • Develops 'champions' who are capable of acting self-sufficiently • Runs interference and fights for resources for his group while passing credit to the individual contributors • Focuses others on priorities by communicating simply and repetitively • Eliminates any irrelevant issues that will cloud the objectives	• Assumes that all subordinates share the same goals and fails to distinguish between different needs, motivations and objectives, using the same techniques to influence everybody • Happier to contribute from a support role than to assume the responsibility for drawing subordinates to him • May try to control subordinates by manipulating benefits rather than empowering them • Does not step into the role of being a potential catalyst for a team effort • Relies on the authority of his position and title to influence subordinates • Introduces too many concurrent directions or critical success factors to keep subordinates focused on key priorities • Loses power by expecting subordinates to commit to more objectives than they can handle

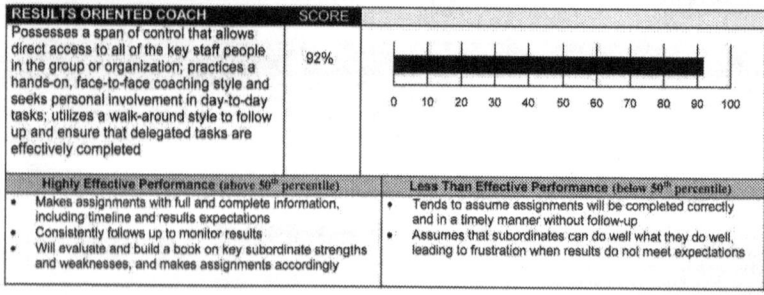

RESULTS ORIENTED COACH	SCORE	
Possesses a span of control that allows direct access to all of the key staff people in the group or organization; practices a hands-on, face-to-face coaching style and seeks personal involvement in day-to-day tasks; utilizes a walk-around style to follow up and ensure that delegated tasks are effectively completed	92%	

Highly Effective Performance (above 50th percentile)	Less Than Effective Performance (below 50th percentile)
• Makes assignments with full and complete information, including timeline and results expectations • Consistently follows up to monitor results • Will evaluate and build a book on key subordinate strengths and weaknesses, and makes assignments accordingly	• Tends to assume assignments will be completed correctly and in a timely manner without follow-up • Assumes that subordinates can do well what they do well, leading to frustration when results do not meet expectations

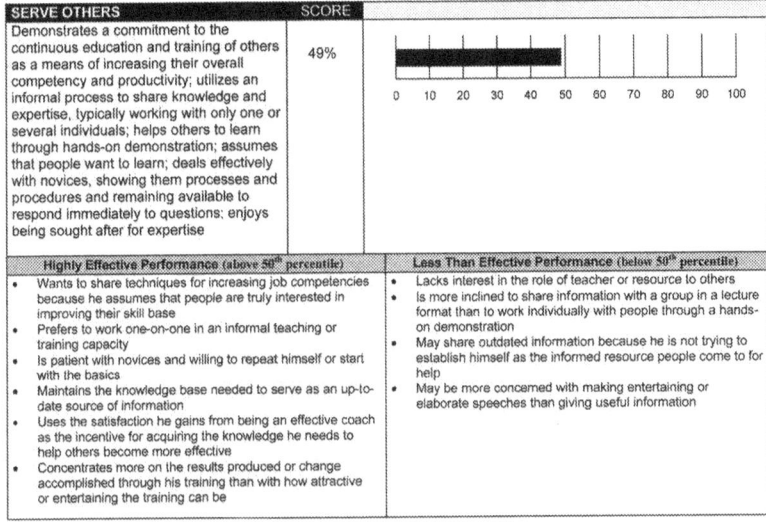

SERVE OTHERS	SCORE	
Demonstrates a commitment to the continuous education and training of others as a means of increasing their overall competency and productivity; utilizes an informal process to share knowledge and expertise, typically working with only one or several individuals; helps others to learn through hands-on demonstration; assumes that people want to learn; deals effectively with novices, showing them processes and procedures and remaining available to respond immediately to questions; enjoys being sought after for expertise	49%	

Highly Effective Performance (above 50th percentile)	Less Than Effective Performance (below 50th percentile)
• Wants to share techniques for increasing job competencies because he assumes that people are truly interested in improving their skill base	• Lacks interest in the role of teacher or resource to others
• Prefers to work one-on-one in an informal teaching or training capacity	• Is more inclined to share information with a group in a lecture format than to work individually with people through a hands-on demonstration
• Is patient with novices and willing to repeat himself or start with the basics	• May share outdated information because he is not trying to establish himself as the informed resource people come to for help
• Maintains the knowledge base needed to serve as an up-to-date source of information	• May be more concerned with making entertaining or elaborate speeches than giving useful information
• Uses the satisfaction he gains from being an effective coach as the incentive for acquiring the knowledge he needs to help others become more effective	
• Concentrates more on the results produced or change accomplished through his training than with how attractive or entertaining the training can be	

THE ASSESSMENT DATABASE

The assessment you recently completed has been intensively developed, validated, and standardized on large samples of successfully employed management, technical, sales, administrative, and other skilled individuals. The database includes over 400,000 individuals.

ASSESSMENT RELIABILITY

The assessment measures motivation and relevant skills you have acquired over time. The results for most people are highly reliable and stable over time. This means that for people who take the assessment, over 90% will have nearly the same results from one year to the next. This does not imply that people cannot change . . . only that most people do not. If, at the age of 20, you like baseball and don't like horror movies, the chances are that at age 60, you'll still like baseball and avoid horror movies. Note, also, that for most people, short-term circumstances usually do not affect the results, i.e., having a good or bad day will usually not change the scores.

ASSESSMENT ACCURACY

While no assessment can be perfect, our standards for accuracy are quite high. In general, 95% of the people who review their own results feel that the assessment was 95% accurate in describing them. Often, if some part of the results does not seem to fit, it is a good idea to ask a close friend or family member to also review the results. If they agree with the results, it is likely that this is an area you are less conscious of and represents a blind spot in your own self-awareness.

We hope this information has been useful. These questionnaires were developed carefully and represent a modern, scientific method of assessment. The reliability of these results will fade with time since individuals can change. Data more than one year old should be reevaluated.

Recommended Reading for Impact Players

These books are recommended because they value synthesis as well as analysis, emotion, and logic.

The Bible—any version.

Beamer, Lisa, with David Edmonson. *Let's Roll.* Alive Communications Inc, 2002.

Bennis, Warren. *Leaders: The Strategies for Taking Charge.* 2nd ed. Harperbusiness, 1997.

Frankl, Viktor. *Man's Search for Meaning.* Beacon Press, 2000.

Giuliani, Rudolph W., with Ken Kurson. *Leadership.* Miramax, 2002.

Gladwell, Malcolm. *The Tipping Point.* Little Brown & Company, 2000.

Goodin, Seth. *The Purple Cow.* Portfolio, 2003.

Hamel, Gary. *Leading the Revolution.* Highbridge Company, 2000.

Hammond, Grant. *The Mind of War.* Smithsonian Institution, 2001.

Heifetz, Ronald A., and Marty Linsky. *Leadership on the Line.* Harvard Business School Publishing, 2002.

Jenkins, Roy. *Churchill: A Biography.* First Plume Printing, 2002.

Kubler-Ross, Elisabeth. *On Death & Dying.* Scribner, 1997. (Reprint)

Meili, Trisha. *I Am the Central Park Jogger.* Scribner, 2003.

Sanders, Tim. *Love Is the Killer App.* Crown Business, 2002.

Swonk, Diane. *The Passionate Economist.* John Wiley & Sons, 2003.

Traum, Dick. *A Victory for Humanity*. Wrs Publishing, 1993.

Useem, Michael. *The Leadership Moment*. Random House Inc, 1998.

Welch, Jack, with John A. Byrne. *Jack Straight from the Gut*. Warner Books Inc, 2001.

Connect the Dot Illustrations

The Following Illustrations Recap the Major Tenets of the Book

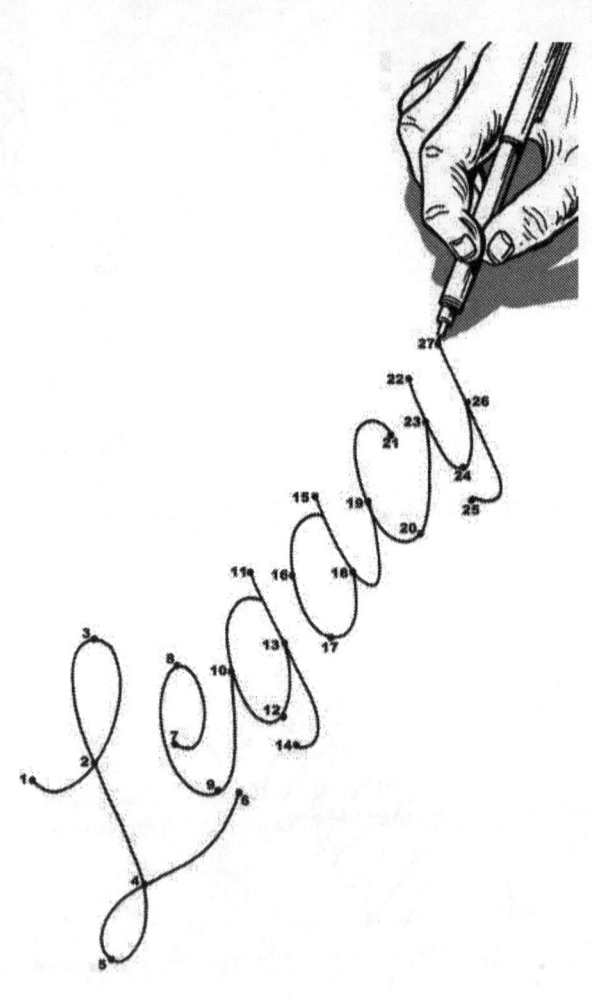

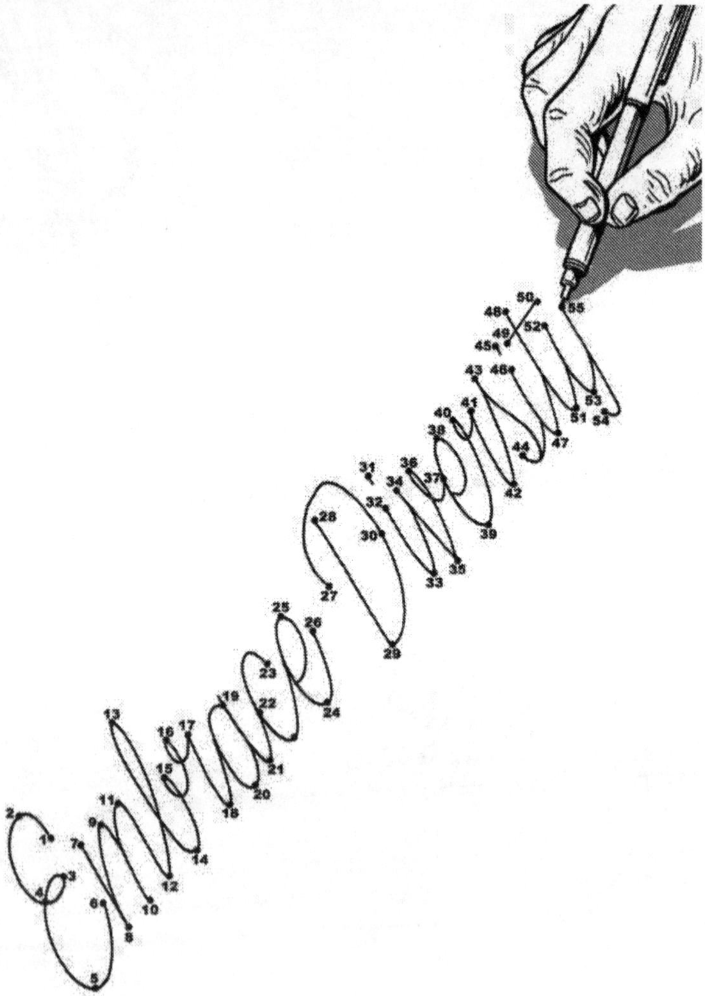

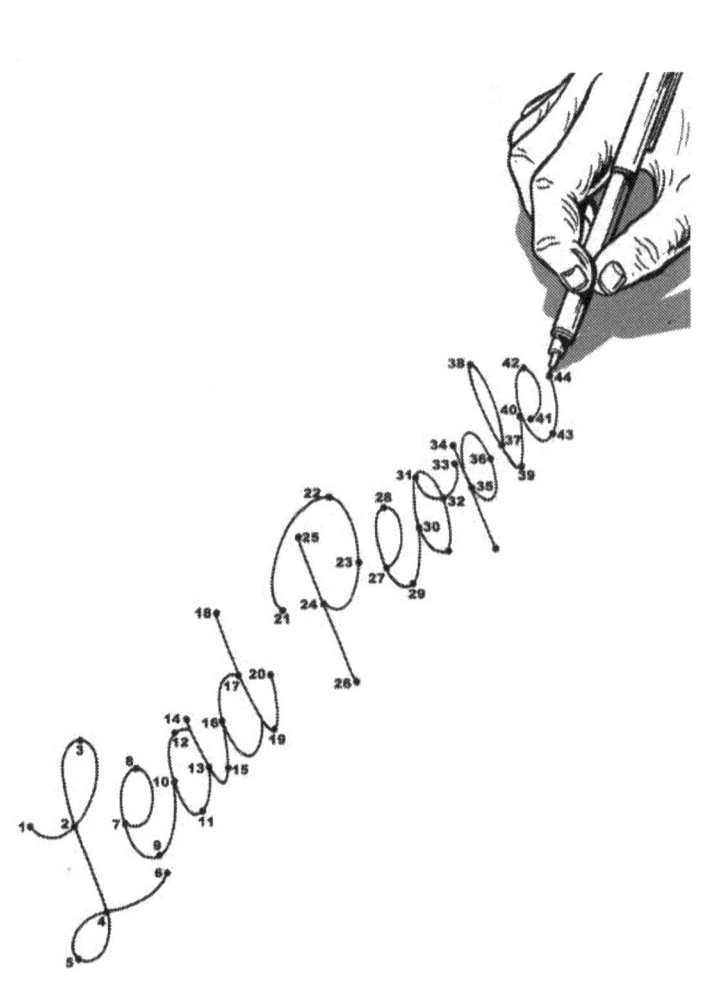

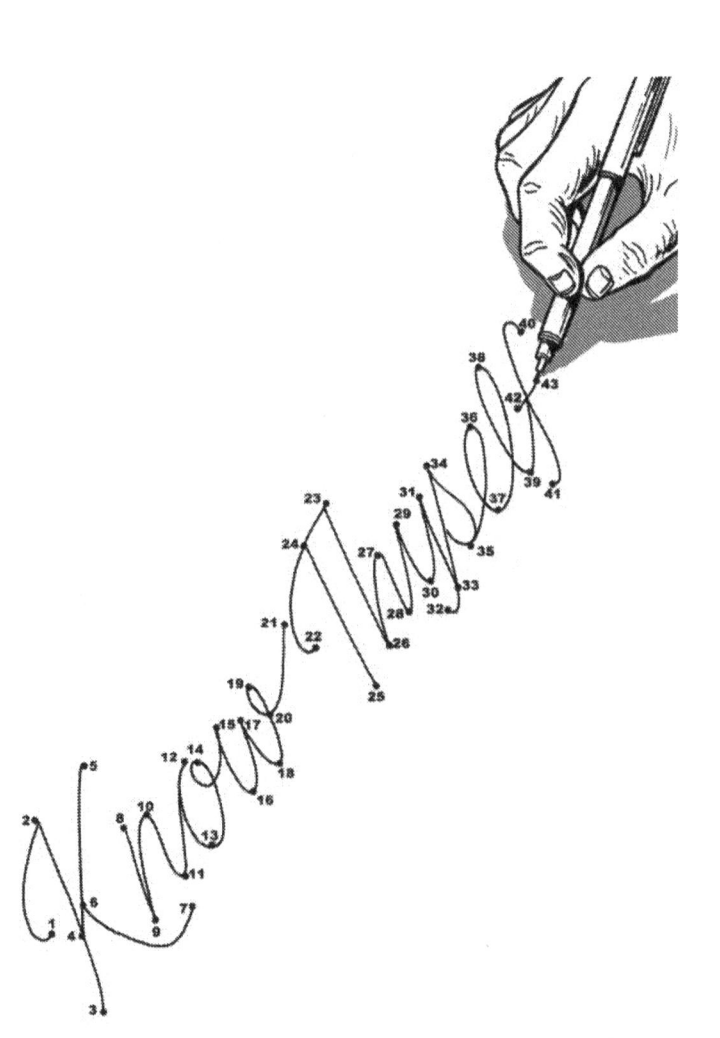

About the Author

Dick Lynch is the founder of the Impact Player Institute and the Impact Player League. His leadership conferences have attracted CEOs, congressmen, professional athletes, and executives from Fortune-500 companies including General Motors, Procter & Gamble, EDS, and Bank of America. He had his own show on Clear Channel radio. He graduated from Brown University with a degree in Organizational Behavior. Dick is married to Karen and they have four wonderful children.

0-595-29492-8

www.ingramcontent.com/pod-product-compliance
Lightning Source LLC
Chambersburg PA
CBHW020735180526
45163CB00001B/243